History of Roman Literature

History of Roman Literature

LUDWIG BIELER

Professor of Palaeography and Late Latin
at University College, Dublin

CONDENSED AND ADAPTED FROM
THE GERMAN, WITH THE COLLA-
BORATION OF THE AUTHOR, BY

JOHN WILSON

MACMILLAN · *London* · *Melbourne* · *Toronto*
ST MARTIN'S PRESS · New York · 1966

MACMILLAN AND COMPANY LIMITED
Little Essex Street London WC2
also Bombay Calcutta Madras Melbourne

THE MACMILLAN COMPANY OF CANADA LIMITED
70 Bond Street Toronto 2

ST MARTIN'S PRESS INC
175 Fifth Avenue New York NY 10010

Library of Congress catalog card number 66–14851

PRINTED IN GREAT BRITAIN

Contents

Preface

A CRITIC of my *Geschichte der Römischen Literatur*, Mr. Robert Browning of University College, London, expressed the wish that my performance should, with appropriate modifications, be repeated in English (*The Classical Review*, 1962, p. 66). The present volume is my response to this suggestion.

The modifications which my book has undergone until it received its final form have been considerable. It was agreed that the English edition should cater for a wider public than that of the German original. I had set out to write a vade-mecum for university students and for academic colleagues who were not classical scholars. The English version, it is hoped, will be found useful by everyone who is interested in the classics, particularly by classics teachers of all levels, and perhaps also by the more ambitious among their pupils. Accordingly, a certain amount of minor detail and all references to learned controversy as well as the bibliographical notes had to be sacrificed. Sidelights on the literatures of modern Europe have been limited to such a range as would seem to fall within the scope of secondary education. Quotations in Latin are followed by an English translation.

The adaptation along these lines has been the work of Mr. John Wilson, of King's School, Canterbury. For the translation, Mr. Wilson and I take an equal share of responsibility. At the final stage, Mr. Browning kindly agreed to read the galley proofs, and made a number of suggestions for improvement, which have been incorporated. I take this opportunity of expressing my deep gratitude for the incentive he has given me, and for his active interest in the progress of this publication.

A revised edition of the German original was published in 1965. Wherever my revision concerns a matter of some importance the English version has been altered accordingly.

The publishers suggested that this book should include some illustrations. I welcomed the idea and submitted a selection-choosing not only portraits of authors and pages from manu, scripts of their works, but also two details from the Ara Pacis, which, in my opinion, capture admirably the spirit of Augustan Rome.

May this book help many readers to realize that the poets and writers of ancient Rome are something more than great names that now as in the past they can stimulate our minds, can move and charm us.

LUDWIG BIELER

List of Plates

*The publishers gratefully acknowledge permission
to reproduce the photographs obtained
from the sources shown*

1. Introduction

THE terms 'Roman literature' and 'Latin literature' overlap. Latin continued to be spoken and written for a long time after the Roman Empire in the West had declined. In the states which grew up on Roman territory, Latin remained the language of literature; from the time of Charlemagne it existed as the universal and unifying language alongside the languages of the national literatures. It is still the language of the Roman Catholic Church.

Not all Romans wrote Latin. The first annalists wrote Greek, and so, occasionally, did Cicero and others. In older times Italians like Plautus and Ennius, or an African like Terence, made themselves a name in Roman literature; and so too, at a later date, did some Greeks and Easterners, to whom Latin was not their mother tongue. But from the classical period onwards, those parts of the Roman world which actively contributed to its literature were thoroughly Romanized. The bulk of Roman literature is the literary creation of men who came from the Romanized provinces; native citizens of Rome are but little represented except in oratory. Thus it is the Italians and later the provincials who proclaim what is Roman. That goes for Ennius in the second century B.C. no less than for Rutilius Namatianus in the fifth century A.D.

A definition of our subject is necessary as regards contents. To exclude all that is not 'belles-lettres' is scarcely justifiable for the historian of a modern literature, even less so for the historian of an ancient one. Purely technical writing can claim only a modest space here; but there are three fields of learning which antiquity considered essential to culture and hence counted as 'literature' — history, philosophy and rhetoric. In a world

I

which saw the essay, novel and short story only in their beginnings, historical writing, philosophical dialogue and the theory
of rhetoric (which partly took the place of our literary criticism)
were, together with oratory itself, the principal forms of literary
prose.

A borderline case is the Latin literature of the Ancient Church.
Neither can it be treated here exhaustively and in its own right,
nor must it be entirely omitted. At the end of antiquity, Roman
literature became Christian. As Latin Christian literature it
handed on the ancient heritage to the middle ages.

THE CHARACTER OF ROMAN LITERATURE

Among the peoples of Ancient Italy, the Romans alone created
a literature. This is not to say that formal language, falling into
rhythmical patterns, was unknown outside Rome; but elsewhere
no literature grew from it. The Italics wrote poetry and prose
in the language of Rome, who was mistress of Italy even before
she had a literature of her own.

But Roman literature is not an Italian literature, which would
have looked quite different. Temperamentally, the ancient
Italians differed but little from the Italians of today, and the
Romans would not have been too different from their neighbours. Nevertheless, the literature of this people is from beginning to end unmistakably Roman, and has a spirit and character
of its own. This is all the more remarkable in view of the fact
that many of the earlier Latin authors did not write in their
native language. There are, of course, degrees of assimilation.
The Latin of Plautus allows some comparison with the French
of a Breton; the Latin of Terence, who writes the idiom not of
a people, but of a social group, may be compared to the French
of an educated Russian of the eighteenth century. Strangely
enough, the Romans did not give their language their own name.
The *populus Romanus*, and later the Roman Empire, spoke Latin;
but the ancient literature in the Latin language is Roman.

Roman literature has a unique standing among the literatures of the world. Whoever judges it only by literary or aesthetic standards may not reckon it among the greatest. It has few names of the rank of Homer or Sophocles, Thucydides or Plato, Shakespeare, Cervantes, Goethe or Dostoevski. On the other hand, Roman literature is universal like no other; nor has any other literature had such a wide and lasting effect. Without Roman literature there would be no Romance literatures, and no English prose. Even in German literature the greatest names are deeply indebted to the Latin school. Greek influence was felt in sporadic encounters; Roman influence runs through the centuries like a mighty river. Contact with the Greeks acted as a powerful (sometimes overpowering) stimulus; the Roman heritage was for one generation after the other its daily bread.

Roman literature is the one universal literature of antiquity. It had at its disposal all the talent of the Mediterranean world: Greeks, Etruscans, Gauls, Africans. Above all, it absorbed the great Greek literature which preceded it. To the European middle ages, Greek mythology, Greek thought, Greek science came almost exclusively through the Romans. Roman literature is more uniform than is Greek literature. The literary forms of the Greeks are linguistically differentiated: epic, lyric, drama and science preserve in the main the dialect in which each form first developed. Roman literature has one language for all forms, but from the beginning differentiates them through style. Roman literature is ecumenical. From its first blossoming it is the literature of a world empire — an empire in the making, at the height of its power, in progressive decline. But before it comes to its end, 'Roman' literature becomes 'Latin' literature, the literature of a spiritual kingdom which outlasts the disintegration of the Western empire.

The 'originality' of Roman literature has often been questioned. It would perhaps be more appropriate to inquire into its spontaneity, as originality did not become a criterion of artistic value until the late eighteenth century. Among the Greeks we witness the birth of a literature in its own right. This is an unparalleled phenomenon, at least in the ancient world. We see how, in Greek literature, one form after the other reaches its historically conditioned perfection, and then dies off. Not so with the Romans. They take over the developed Greek forms, almost all at the same time, as their artistic canons, but fill them with a new life. This has happened again and again in European literature. Attic tragedy had died out with Euripides. European drama, from Ennius and Pacuvius to the mystery and morality plays of the middle ages and from there right up to Ibsen and Sartre, is each time reborn in a new spirit. The Greek heroic epic begins and ends for us with Homer (what follows him is either decline or artificial revival). The Roman epic, whose first master introduces himself as a reincarnation of Homer, has almost as many rebirths as there are poets : Ennius, Vergil, Lucan and so on through the middle ages to Dante, then again from the epics of the early Renaissance among the Italians, the Portuguese, the English, to the prose-epic of modern times, the large-scale novel.

One must distinguish between the formal conventions of a literary genre and what is expressed in it. The Romans took over Greek forms because the Greeks at the height of their culture had developed them to such perfection that it seemed hopeless to put anything better in their place. But the Romans differed from the Greeks in their attitude to these forms. A Greek writer would move with individual freedom in the conventions of the genre which he had chosen. Within these limits there was room for personalities as strikingly different as, for example, Sophocles and Euripides. The Roman poet gives every form which he adopts a Roman stamp. He usually tries his hand at more than one genre and readily allows himself a certain compromise, a mixture of conventions and styles ; he handles forms more elastically, more ' openly '. He does not create new basic forms, but in his work adopted forms enter into new combinations. In this sense Roman literature, too, is creative.

Many nations of the ancient world came into contact with Greek culture — Phrygians, Armenians, Thracians, Egyptians, Etruscans, Oscans, Celts. At the time of the decisive encounter most of these were on more or less the same, if not on a higher, level of civilization than the Romans; they knew the use of writing and had the rudiments of a literature. But only the Romans felt the urge towards a national culture on the Greek pattern. The practical, level-headed Roman without cultural interests, without a sense of beauty, is not the whole picture.

However, the Roman often sought to suppress the artistic side of his nature. In the earliest times this was a law of necessity, later a hallowed convention of society. Cicero himself, man of letters and connoisseur, felt obliged (like the modern Englishman) to play the dilettante; the spirit of the society into which he was born had so much power over him that, against his nature, he entered into the career of a politician and gave in to his literary inclinations only in times of involuntary leisure.

The literature of the Romans grows up between two extremes: the rudiments of a popular literature which Rome shares with the Italian tribes, and the masterpieces of the Greeks. The Italian element was able to develop but little. Roman *gravitas*, if it did not quite suppress it, gave it next to no chance. It remains an undercurrent, which only occasionally comes to the surface, as, *e.g.*, in the 'Latin' comedy of the Plautine type. To Greek culture, on the other hand, victorious Rome surrendered almost without opposition, readily, yet neither unconditionally nor indiscriminately; and what the Roman took over, he transformed in the spirit of that *humanitas* which we see expressed in its most perfect form in the circle of the younger Scipio and in the literary work of Cicero.

THE SURVIVAL OF ROMAN LITERATURE

To the modern observer, Roman literature seems like a site of ruins; only here and there a monument towers intact or but lightly damaged. Of nearly eight hundred Latin authors of the ancient world whose names are known, scarcely more than a fifth speak to us from at least one surviving work; we have fragments of about one half of those authors; the rest are mere names. Among the losses are works as outstanding as Cato's *Origines*, Cicero's *Hortensius*, the elegies of Cornelius Gallus, and the *Thyestes* of Varius. Whole schools and genres are almost entirely lost for us. Of the drama in Roman dress (*fabula praetexta* and *fabula togata*), of the mime, of the *Atellanae*, of the annals under Sulla, of the 'new' poetry in the environment of Catullus, we can only form the vaguest idea. Even the reconstruction of the *Annals* of Ennius, the *Satires* of Lucilius, and the *Histories* of Sallust, of which there are numerous fragments, is problematical in detail.

Most of the casualties occurred towards the end of antiquity. The most general reason was the decline of culture, and the destruction and dispersion of many libraries in the almost unbroken series of wars and invasions. Looted manuscripts would easily come to harm; the incomplete copies were often sold as discards and found their way into monasteries where there was a shortage of writing material; there the old writing was roughly obliterated and other texts that were needed were written on top (*codices rescripti*, or palimpsests).

The Christian Church was in itself no enemy of ancient literature; it even included much of it in its cultural programme. The value of pagan literature for the literal and historical understanding of Holy Scripture was recognized at an early date, and so a place was given to the ancient authors, though not without reservations. Open enmity against the classics as on the part of Gregory the Great was rare. The philosophical writings of Cicero, the stoicism of Seneca, the poetry of Vergil (whose fourth *Eclogue* was soon interpreted as Messianic) were commonly understood as foreshadowing Christian thought. Even works to which a Christian might reasonably object were not always destroyed, otherwise we would not possess the didactic poem of the epicurean Lucretius, Ovid's *Art of Love* or substantial portions of the satirical novel of Petronius. Christian thinking did have considerable influence on the choice of what was worth preserving. It must have been all the more effective for the coincidence of the official recognition of Christianity and the flowering of Latin theology in the fourth century with the transition from the papyrus scroll to the parchment codex (which was the model of our printed book). In the process of transfer into the new, handier book form, a good deal of literature no longer considered of interest was thrown overboard. In some circles, however, this transcription was made the occasion for a painstaking revision of pagan and Christian classics.

There were many other reasons for a selection from the mass of literature, involving potential danger for the survival of the rejects. Such forces had been at work already before the ascent of Christianity. The better is always the enemy of the good; in antiquity, when imitation was a principle, not to say a requirement, a masterpiece of its genre often put its forerunners so much into the shade that in course of time they were forgotten. The *Aeneid* of Vergil and the *Satires* of Horace were to replace the works of Ennius and Lucilius; the Augustan poets knew what they owed to their predecessors, but they also knew that the poets of the Republic no longer satisfied contemporary tastes. Ennius and Lucilius found fewer and fewer readers; at the end of antiquity they were not transcribed in *codices*. Were it not for the archaizing tendencies of Hadrian's time, they would have been entirely lost.

The tendency to drop the less perfect is at its strongest in school. A good teacher wants his pupils to imitate only the very best; perhaps he will expressly warn them against the not so perfect, as did Quintilian, under the Flavians, against the then fashionable style of Seneca: the effects of Quintilian's Ciceronianism has been felt almost to the present day. Even if the schools of the West apparently did not have so strictly canonical a selection as we find in the East, they undoubtedly did make a selection, and with the decline in the general culture, the change in the social structure and the difficult times through which the ancient world was passing, the range of school reading constantly narrowed. Quintilian gives characteristics of some fifty Latin poets and writers; the grammarian Arusianus Messius in the fourth century takes his examples from only four authors: Vergil, Terence, Sallust and Cicero.

Certainly there were men right to the end of antiquity who were widely read in Roman literature, *e.g.* Sidonius Apollinaris in the fifth century or Boethius on the threshold of the sixth; but they are only the peaks of a sinking world. Some texts which came down to the middle ages in only one copy, such as Cicero's treatise *On the State*, or the selections from Petronius, have possibly survived by chance. Occasionally, there might have been a special motive; our Catullus text, for example, goes back to a single manuscript, now lost, which in the tenth century was still preserved in Verona, the poet's native town.

A great mass of non-Christian Latin writing owes its survival to the requirements of daily life. Most of it is 'practical literature', often in pedestrian or un-literary language: technical works like the Architecture of Vitruvius (Augustan era), the books of Vegetius on military techniques and veterinary medicine, writings of late antiquity on agriculture and surveying. A human need is served also by medicine; here the Romans are directly influenced by the Greeks, from the medicine of Celsus to the late Latin translations of Greek works.

One particular reason for the loss of voluminous works is the popular practice, in use from the third century A.D., of epitomization, a fore-runner of our shortened editions and book digests. Not every reader had the patience and leisure to study the one hundred and forty-two books of Livy's Roman history; extracts were made at an early date, and distributed through book dealers. In the third and fourth centuries these extracts shrank to scanty compendiums. The fate of Livy's work is well known: of his one hundred and forty-two books we now possess only thirty-five.

SOURCES FOR ROMAN LITERARY HISTORY

The most important sources for Roman literary history are the surviving works. Their study is the first task of the literary historian, which nothing can replace. But we are not content to understand a work of literature as a linguistic document, evaluate it aesthetically and grasp its message; we want also to understand it historically, as a creation of its author, as a conditioned and conditioning element of his cultural and intellectual, political and social situation, as a stage of development of a literary form, as an expression of an artistic tendency.

Here is our first difficulty. An ancient author hardly ever reveals himself in his work directly, and the ancient biographer, with his preference for anecdotic clichés, seldom describes those personal traits which could give us some insight into the creative process behind a writer's work. Exceptions (*e.g.* the lives of Terence, Vergil and Horace from the *De Poetis* of Suetonius) allow us to divine what in many other instances we may have missed. There we learn some particulars of Vergil's methods of working, or glance at the correspondence of Augustus with Horace and Maecenas.

Most ancient authors hide behind their works, but a few do tell us something about themselves. What sort of picture would we have of Cicero's personality without his letters to Atticus? Horace in his *Satires* and *Epistles*, and in many odes also, speaks to us as a man and poet almost with the directness of a contemporary; we even know his personal style of living. The poetic autobiography of Ovid (*Trist.* 4, 1) is written with great subtlety of psychological observation. Nevertheless, what Roman authors, especially the earlier ones, tell about themselves concerns mostly facts of their external lives — the composition of their works or some personally decisive events, such as the conferment of civil rights on Ennius or Vergil's loss of his paternal estate. Not until the end of antiquity do we find an example of self-analysis, in the modern manner, in the *Confessions* of St. Augustine; Christianity opened up a new dimension of the inner life. In a work of literature, the use of the first person need not of course imply that the author is making a personal confession; thus the attempts to reconstruct the 'love stories' of Catullus, Tibullus and Propertius out of their poems were destined to failure owing to the very nature of ancient poetry.

Occasionally, one writer refers to another. The ancients already discovered in the *Miles gloriosus* of Plautus an allusion to the dispute of the poet Naevius with the Metelli and his punishment. Propertius hints at the birth of the *Aeneid* as early as the year 26 B.C., although the poem remained unpublished until after Vergil's death in the year 19 B.C. Livy has left us, in a precious fragment of the lost 120th book, a vivid report of Cicero's last day; the letters of the younger Pliny contain interesting news about his friend Tacitus; the elder Seneca (at the beginning of the Empire) put on record memories of Ovid's rhetorical studies, which add characteristic details to the self-portrait of the poet.

The ancient grammarians already worked on this material, and with methods essentially similar to ours. They were in a better position than we are, for at that time most of the texts were still complete. Statements and opinions of grammarians and rhetoricians are often the only sources of our knowledge of lost works. We can, however, test and appraise the working methods of these scholars on the originals which have survived, and thus evaluate more accurately their testimony especially when the latter is supported by quotations.

A scientific philology developed in Rome from the middle of the second century B.C. Its first great representative is L. Aelius Stilo, in the time of Sulla. One of the tasks Roman literary scholars set themselves was the surveying of archaic literature and the establishment of its chronology. Some dates were furnished by official records. Tragedies and comedies, which, as in Greece, belonged to the programme of religious feasts, were commissioned by the state. From official sources originate, for example, the *Didascaliae*, which put on record dates and other particulars concerning the performance of dramatic works; we have such *Didascaliae* concerning the comedies of Terence and two comedies of Plautus. In the time of the Gracchi scholars began to take an interest in Plautus, who was particularly popular; the texts of his plays, which circulated only in stage copies, had already got much out of hand, and many plays by others went under his name. The texts were then fixed as far as possible; but not until Varro, a contemporary of Cicero, were twenty-one Plautine comedies singled out of the mass as indisputably genuine; with the exception of the last, they have come down to us, almost unimpaired, as a collected edition. Varro also included in his *Imagines* — portraits of famous Romans with accompanying text — the older poets and authors, and Cornelius Nepos, a man of the same generation, in his only partially surviving work *De viris illustribus*, gave, *inter alia*, biographies of Roman orators and historians.

This, certainly, is not literary history as we understand it; but in the ancient world literary history in our sense did not exist. Writing about the lives of authors fell under the genre of biography; lists of works, questions of authenticity and studies of language were the affair of the grammarian; aesthetic criticism was mainly a concern of the *rhetor*, and the nature of literary forms and their origins was a part of philosophy. A synthesis of these aspects, let alone a historical study of the national literature, was never contemplated. There are, of course, no rigid barriers between the several ways of approach. Thus the poem *De poetis* of Volcacius Sedigitus (at the turn of the second to the first century) combined biographical matter with aesthetic judgements; and Cicero's *Brutus*, our most important source on earlier Roman eloquence, contains, besides the rhetorical characterization of orators, many details of a personal nature.

Unfortunately, Roman literary history has shared the fate of its object. Very little remains: Cicero's *Brutus*, the biographies of Cato and Atticus by Cornelius Nepos, the collection of rhetorical specimens of the elder Seneca, Quintilian, and from the *Virorum illustrium libri* of Suetonius the excerpt *De grammaticis et rhetoribus*. The complete work of Suetonius was still known in the fourth century. Donatus drew from it the biographies which he prefaced to his commentary on Terence and his lost commentary on Vergil. Donatus's pupil, Jerome, not only inserted numerous extracts from Suetonius in his Latin treatment of the world-chronicle of Eusebius; he even wrote, in imitation of Suetonius, under the title of *De viris illustribus*, a summary of Christian literary history, which was continued by Gennadius of Marseilles, at the end of the fifth century, and Isidore of Seville, who died in A.D. 636.

Suetonius concludes the section on grammarians with an appreciation of M. Valerius Probus, a man whose work, little noticed by his contemporaries, became of great importance for the critical establishment of the older classical texts and their grammatical understanding. He came from Berytos (Beirut) and seems to have lived until about the end of the first century. At a time when earlier literature had gone out of fashion in the capital and was scarcely taught in the schools any longer, Probus gathered together old texts in the provinces (where people were always more conservative), purged them of errors, added critical signs after the Alexandrian fashion, and noted peculiarities of idiom. He published very little, on special questions only, and nothing of any great length. He never had more than two or three pupils at a time; by informal conversation he initiated them into his interests and his method. Their own work along such lines must have contributed much to the literary archaism of the second century. The antiquarian Aulus Gellius (born about A.D. 130) knew pupils of Probus personally. Probus himself does not seem to have written any regular commentaries but traces of his textual criticism are found in commentaries on Vergil and in the Terence commentary of Donatus.

Commentaries were above all necessary in school; many commentaries on school authors go back to a rather early time.

Whether the explanations were originally written in the margins of the texts (as in the manuscripts of the middle ages) is unknown; most commentaries were probably published as independent works, especially when they were concerned less with linguistic and factual explanations than with the general background for the historical understanding of the text. Such is the commentary on several of Cicero's orations by Asconius Pedianus (first century A.D.), who brought to his task an intimate knowledge of the history of the times. Acro, too, whose lost Horace commentary probably falls in the second century, was still in a position to study the environment of the poet from good sources and especially to identify the people to whom Horace alluded. Alone in its class is the *Commentum Terenti* of Aelius Donatus, which combines a subtle study of the poet's language with aesthetic and dramatic analysis, and illustrates in detail Terence's use of his Greek models. The other commentaries of late antiquity are less interesting to the historian of literature : either they are too pedantically scholastic (like the commentary on Vergil of Ti. Claudius Donatus), or they digress too much into regions which do not help the literary understanding of the text.

Biographers, grammarians, antiquarians and also philosophers are the most important repository for fragments of lost works. The value of such authors as sources is very varied. Cicero quotes often and fully from earlier poetry, especially from his favourite poet, Ennius; he quotes poetry mostly in support of philosophical theses or as rhetorical examples. This has for us the advantage that we often get to know longer passages. Aulus Gellius in the second century, Censorinus in the third, and Macrobius at the beginning of the fifth century also often quote at some length. The grammatical textbooks, on the other hand (most influential were Aelius Donatus in the fourth century and Priscian at about A.D. 500), quote only for linguistic reasons and without interest in the larger context; things are even worse in the *Compendiosa doctrina* of Nonius Marcellus, who is interested merely in philological and antiquarian rarities.

2. Roman Literature
up to 133 B.C.

CONDITIONS for the origin of a literature must have been the same in Rome as in the rest of Italy. The primitive Roman community would have the same collective needs as its near and far neighbours. Yet it had experienced early, and more so than most of the other communities, alien influences from several quarters. Rome not only had much immigration from surrounding tribes — the Romulus of legend declared his town an asylum — and continually absorbed with the spread of its power new Italic elements; it was from the beginning overshadowed by two superior civilizations, the Etruscan and the Greek.

The nature and degree of this influence are difficult to ascertain. Numerous 'culture words', which reflect an upper-class way of life, were borrowed from the Etruscans. The many Etruscan family names in Rome speak even more clearly of the Etruscan element in that city; Roman legend bears witness to the Etruscan origin of the Tarquins. Even the name of Rome seems to be Etruscan; perhaps it was Etruscans who transformed the settlement on the Tiber into a town. Etruscan influence is very noticeable in religious and state ceremonial: in the lictors who accompanied the king and later the highest officials and priests; in the triumph (including the strangling of the defeated leaders); in the ancestor-worship of the aristocratic families with their ancestral images (*imagines*), which were worn as masks at solemn funerals; in the inspection of entrails and other ritual which the Romans summarized as *disciplina Tusca*. The blood-thirsty gladiatorial games, first seen in Rome at the funeral of

14

D. Iunius Pera, 264 B.C., were also of Etruscan origin; the Etruscan religion knew human sacrifice, and when Rome in historical times occasionally for special reasons sacrificed human beings, the Etruscan practice was followed closely. After the power of the Etruscans had been broken, Rome would minimize their significance for her own past; but those who had Etruscan blood in their veins, like Maecenas, were proud of the fact. The Etruscan upper-class, however, had been numerically too small to leave a strong imprint on the Roman character; and in Roman literature, besides the dilettante Maecenas, only two Etruscans are found, the satirist Persius in the time of Nero and the late elegist Maximianus.

The influence of the Greeks goes much deeper, although it is not at first so tangible. Rome was open to Greek influence long before she became a political power in the hellenistic world. Indirect Greek influence was exercised through the Etruscans, whose culture owed so much to the Greeks, and also through the Southern Italians, especially the Oscans, who had close connexions with the towns of 'Greater Greece' but who had also come under Etruscan power. For example, the Romans called some Greek gods and heroes by their Etruscan names; also the word *persona* (originally meaning 'mask') is (according to Devoto) the Greek *prosopon* borrowed indirectly through the Etruscan *fersu*. Contact with Greek culture is suggested in the report of the origin of the Twelve Tables (Liv. III, 31) and confirmed by a comparative study of legal history; Greek religious songs might have shaped even the oldest Latin sacred poetry; and the 'saturnian' line, despite its Italian name, has Greek parallels.

The nature and origin of the saturnian verse are contested. The line is Italic, not exclusively Roman. It cannot be proved to be either purely quantitative or purely accentuating. The earliest examples show great diversity of form and freedom of handling. The stress seems to follow the accent of the clause; yet the nature of the earliest Latin accent is just as problematic as that of the saturnian.

The saturnian is a long line, related to the long lines of other Indo-European languages. Of its halves the first often has a rising, the second a falling, rhythm. The opening line of Livius Andronicus may serve as an example:

Virum mihi Camēna insecē versutum

The Romans could have come to know Greek lines analogous to the saturnian in Southern Italy.

Those set forms of speech from which literature develops are universally linked at first to particular occasions, or serve particular requirements of life. Speech can only become 'literature' when the oral tradition is recorded; but the orally communicated poetry, narrative art and teaching also had a long way to go before they reached their known stages.

In the language of every community we find, along with the unmetrical speech of everyday intercourse, the metrical, formulary speech — as an 'answer' to typical situations, and as a formulation of typical, and thus potentially collective, experience. It is a form of elevated speech in which verse and rhythmic prose are often not yet clearly differentiated. Since archaic ways of life are rigid and ritualistic, archaic language consists largely of such formulae. This was especially true of the conservative Roman, who upheld that formality in religion and law, in public and in private life much longer than the Greeks. This formality (*gravitas*) remained a customary attitude long after it had ceased to be a ritual.

Formulary language was known to the Romans as *carmen*. This word embraced in the older times not only (according to the definition of Servius) 'what is composed in verse' (*quidquid pedibus continetur*), but everything that was expressed in formal speech (*conceptis verbis*): prayer and charm, legal maxim and proverb, solemn pronouncements of officials and priests, and of course the song, which later, under Greek influence, became the 'poem'.

An old Roman prayer, which was spoken by the father of the house during the annual procession along the boundaries of his estate in spring, has been preserved for us by Cato. There we find rhythmic structure, asyndeton, triple groups with -*que* in the last element, alliteration and rhyme, and, finally, recurring lines and patterns which articulate and organize the whole. The Salian priesthood of Mars held in March and October, at the beginning and end of the agricultural year, processions with festive dancing and songs. We actually know the song of the Fratres Arvales, priests of Dea Dia, a goddess of the countryside, whose festival was celebrated in May. The text of the song is contained in a record of this priesthood from the year A.D. 218; its archaic wording was by then already unintelligible, and has yielded its meaning only to modern linguistic science. The metre is the saturnian. The song is concluded by a five times' recurring *triumpe*. Joyful shouts of *io triump(h)e* were uttered also at the triumphal procession, which originally was a ritual.

In the religious sphere also belong the 'conjurations' (*indigitamenta*) of divine beings. One step further and we are in the world of charms, specimens of which survive in the works of some late authors. A magic act from ancient times is the death consecration (*devotio*): the Roman general, in the moment of utmost danger, consecrated himself and the enemy to the gods of the underworld; then he sought death in battle, so as to involve the enemy in his own downfall. The words of the death consecration which Livy puts in the mouth of P. Decius Mus (in the battle at Vesuvius, 340 B.C.) render, in slightly modernized language, an old formula of 'devotion'.

The Romans certainly had war-songs, working songs and cradle songs; later authors presume their existence, but next to nothing survives. We know only indirectly about the suggestive *Versus Fescennini* which were improvised at wedding feasts. The name *Fescennini* (from the Faliscan town of Fescennium in Etruria) points to something which was borrowed from abroad, but the custom as such seems to have been native to the Romans.

Similar is the case of the improvised drama, the Italian farce. It certainly was as autochthonous in Rome as elsewhere, and yet was called *ludus Oscus, fabula Atellana*. The special form practised in Rome must thus have come from the Oscan town of Atella.

Besides the *Atellanae*, which were played by Roman citizens, there was the theatre of the professional actors (*histriones*). Livy, clearly following earlier learned tradition, traced its origins far back : in 364 B.C. Etruscan dancers were called to Rome and performed ritual dances to avert a plague ; their performance found favour, and the *ludi* were kept on beyond their original occasion. However this may be, the later *ludi scaenici* are clearly in the theatrical tradition of the Greeks. It is conceivable that adaptations of Greek plays were performed in Etruria, but we have no information about this. The word *histrio*, however, is Etruscan.

Experience was passed on from father to son, for example, the 'peasant rule' *hiberno pulvere verno luto grandia farra, Camille, metes* ('From winter dust and spring rain, Camillus, you will reap a big crop of grain'). Norms of conduct are expressed in the sentences (*praecepta*) of a sage (*vates*), of no fixed time and perhaps legendary, called Marcius ; for example, *postremus dicas, primus taceas* — 'Be the last to speak, the first to be silent'.

The norm of conduct of the citizen body is the law. Old law texts were couched in *formulae* everywhere, and especially so in Rome. As late as Cicero's time Roman schoolboys had to learn by heart the Twelve Tables, theoretically the source of all Roman law. The text of these laws was written on twelve bronze tablets when the old customary law, whose administration had long been a privilege of the patricians, was published at the demand of the plebs. The codification is said to have taken place under the auspices of the decemvir Appius Claudius (451–450 B.C.) ; but the text, as quoted by later writers, was probably edited in about 300 B.C. by the censor of the same name.

An age-old custom is the praise of the dead. Its chief forms at Rome were the dirge (*naenia*) and the funeral oration (*laudatio funebris*). The lasting memory of the dead is preserved by the *tituli* under the ancestral images and by sepulchral inscriptions; we still possess the inscriptions on the tombs of several of the Scipios, beginning with L. Cornelius Scipio Barbatus (cos. 298 B.C.), and epigrams on famous poets such as Naevius and Ennius, the latter, according to Cicero, composed by the poet himself. The praise of the dead was also sung at banquets; one would think of these *carmina* as catches, roundelays, or as short poems like the attic *skolion*, rather than as ballads.

As the families preserved the memory of their ancestors so it was customary to record publicly certain events which affected the entire community. The chief priest (*pontifex maximus*) recorded memorable happenings from year to year on a white board set up in public. These *Annales*, however, contained scarcely anything which we would call history. They were continued until the late Republic. At the time of the Gracchi the Pontifex Maximus P. Mucius Scaevola edited them in eighty books as *Annales Maximi*. The title Annales was taken over by the historians.

More important records were contained in the official books (*commentarii*) of the magistrates and priests and the acts of the senate; these, however, were not intended for publication. Caesar, for political purposes, was the first to order the publication of the acts of the senate; he himself, in his *Commentarii*, turned the official report into a work of literature.

Records of such a kind might have contained a germ of literary development but they were not literature. They were not written with a view to a public; and this is just as true of the family archives as of the official books of the priests and magistrates. 'Literature' was created when an individual presented his work for publication. This step was taken by APPIUS CLAUDIUS CAECUS. This great statesman (censor 312 B.C., constructor of the Via Appia, and speaker against the peace with Pyrrhus in 280 B.C.) was also an innovator in that he grasped the value of the written word in public life. As a jurist he had caused his client, the aedile Cn. Flavius, to publish the *Fasti* (legal calendar) and the forms of legal action (*legis actiones*) ; he himself had written on a legal question, *De usurpationibus*.

Appius went even one step further. Although in the early days of Rome the art of poetry was not honoured, and whoever devoted himself to it was regarded as an idler, Appius did not find it beneath his dignity to compose a poem. It took the form of maxims of practical wisdom and so kept within good Roman tradition. Familiarity with philosophical thought is evident in a line of this *carmen*, quoted variously, but not in the original form : 'Every man is the forger of his own luck'.

LIVIUS AND NAEVIUS

Appius Claudius was ahead of his time. Not until a generation after his death do we hear again of a poet in Rome, and he is a Greek.

L. LIVIUS ANDRONICUS is said to have come to Rome as a prisoner of war. His master, a Livy, perhaps the father of M. Livius Salinator (cos. 219 B.C., 207 B.C.), entrusted him with the education of his sons, and as a freedman he founded a school for the sons of the aristocracy. There he interpreted, alongside the standard Greek texts, his translation of Homer's *Odyssey* into Latin saturnians. It was the first poem of some length in the Latin language. The work survived for a long time as a school-book ; even Horace had to learn it under Orbilius. When the saturnian was no longer considered suitable for literature the poem was rewritten in hexameters and at the same time divided into books. Although a literal rather than a re-creative transla-tion, sacrificing some of the subtle beauty of the original, and not free from mistranslations, Livius's *Odusia* nevertheless marks an epoch in Roman literature. A Latin poetic language had been created along Greek lines.

Livius was also the only person available to the aediles of 240 B.C., when it had been decided for the first time to produce a Greek tragedy and comedy in a Latin adaptation for the *Ludi Romani* (in September). As a playwright Livius seems to have treated his models much more freely; he took over the Greek dialogue verse and also apparently some lyric metres, but in a form which suited Latin with its strong accent and its wealth of long syllables.

In the year 207 B.C., at a critical moment of the war with Hannibal, Livius was officially commissioned to compose a processional hymn for a chorus of young maidens, to avert threatening omens; in gratitude for the banished danger, the 'poets and actors' (*scribae et histriones*) were recognized by the state as a guild with rights of assembly, having its seat in the temple of Minerva on the Aventine. As, on a similar occasion in the year 200 B.C., the hymn was written by an otherwise unknown P. Licinius Tegula, Livius Andronicus probably died between 207 B.C. and 200 B.C.

His work was still known at the end of the republic, but it no longer found favour. Cicero compared the Latin *Odyssey* with the primitive sculptures of Daedalus and was of the opinion that Livius's plays did not merit a second reading. Livy the historian did not think it worth the trouble to write out the words of the processional hymn of 207 B.C.

The choice of the saturnian for the translation of the *Odyssey* was presumably a stopgap; its very brevity, compared with the hexameter, was a disadvantage. The Latin language was as yet rather intractable for the hexameter; Naevius, too, wrote his epic in saturnians. The annals of Ennius, who introduced the hexameter to Rome, give some idea of the difficulties which had to be overcome, and which even this great poet did not always master. The dialogue verses of drama were easier to imitate, especially in the free treatment which Livius and his followers allowed themselves.

The *Ludi Romani*, at which Livius produced adaptations of Roman plays for the first time in 240 B.C. (he even appeared in them himself), had been an annual festival since 366 B.C. Whether

stage productions were a part of it before 240 B.C. remains unknown. A primitive 'stage show', which was composed, like a
variety programme, of singing, dancing and short scenes, could
well have existed. According to Valerius Maximus, the young
people of Rome were already giving such performances before
364 B.C., when Etruscan dancers first came to Rome. The new
thing in 240 B.C. was, then, the production of a tragedy and a
comedy with a coherent plot on the Greek model. It is scarcely
an accident that this novelty followed immediately after the end
of the first Punic war. The Roman soldiers stationed in Sicily
had had the opportunity to get to know the Greek theatre, which
had been cultivated in Sicily since the time of Hiero, the tyrant
of Syracuse. There it even had a late flowering. Rhinthon,
author of serio-comic plays, lived until 285 B.C. In the choice
of his models Livius already showed the inclination of the later
Roman theatre towards the classical tragedy of the Athenians
(especially Euripides) and the 'new comedy' of Alexander's time
and that of his early successors.

Livius did not satisfy the literary taste of the Ciceronian and
Augustan era; not until the archaists of the second century B.C.
was he again treasured. Our fragments come largely from
Verrius Flaccus, who had antiquarian interests, from Gellius and
Nonius, and from the late grammarian Priscian.

Five years after the first appearance of Livius Andronicus, the
first play of an Italian, CN. NAEVIUS, was produced in 235 B.C.
His birthplace was probably Capua. He had been a soldier in
the first Punic war. During the second Punic war he seems to
have favoured publicly the delaying tactics of Fabius Cunctator
against the aggressive strategy of the Metelli and Scipios. The
frankness of political criticism on the stage, which he had taken
over from the 'old' (Aristophanic) comedy, brought this pug-
nacious man into conflict with the authorities. When in 206 B.C.
Q. Caecilius Metellus had become consul, he declared in a
comedy: *Fato Metelli Romae fiunt consules*, 'It is by fate (not by
merit) that the Metelli are consuls in Rome'. The Metelli

answered by putting up a threatening notice in a public place: *Malum dabunt Metelli Naevio poetae*, 'The Metelli will punish the poet Naevius'. And they fulfilled their threat: on their instigation (one of the praetors that year was also a Metellus), Naevius was arrested, probably on a charge of *mala carmina*, which were forbidden in the Twelve Tables. He allegedly got back his freedom when he recanted in two further comedies, *Ariolus* and *Leon*. Naevius did not refrain from satirizing even Scipio. He was finally banished, and died in African Utica in 201 B.C. or later.

Naevius was also a strong personality as a poet. In comedy he was equal to Plautus; this much the remaining fragments allow us to infer. The titles of his plays suggest that his Greek models were taken not only from the new, but also from the middle comedy. Personally he introduced an element of political satire, which was foreign to the later Greek comedy.

We know most about his comedy *Tarentilla*. In this play two fathers track down their sons who have squandered their inheritance on a frivolous girl in Tarentum. One fragment vividly describes the coquettish tricks of the Tarentine girl. The mention of guests from Praeneste and Lanuvium in the *Ariolus* could also point to an Italian *milieu*; perhaps, despite a Greek parallel to the title, this was a comedy in Roman costume (*fabula togata*). However that may be, the fragments show throughout the characteristic Roman sense of the realistic and comic, the inclination towards local colour, the sketching of characters in their social setting.

For all that we know, Naevius created the national Roman drama, the *fabula praetexta*; it is called after the costume of its heroes, the official dress (*toga praetexta*) of the Roman magistrate, and takes its subjects from Roman myths and history, including the poet's own time. One of the two *praetextae* of Naevius known to us, *Clastidium*, was an act of patriotic homage, celebrating the victory of M. Claudius Marcellus (222 B.C.). The other one, *Lupus*, was a dramatization of the Romulus legend.

Naevius apparently had less inclination for tragedy in the

B

Greek style. Some of his titles betray an interest in the Trojan cycle (*Equos Troianus, Hector proficiscens*) ; the Romans had learnt already to consider themselves descendants of the Trojans.

This is shown also by Naevius's latest work, his epic *Bellum Poenicum*. He tells in the form of a verse chronicle, in plain yet effective language, the story of the first Punic war, in which he had taken part. He probably made use also of historical sources, like the work of the pro-Carthaginian Philinos of Agrigentum, and perhaps the Greek *Annals* of Q. Fabius Pictor ; but it is the personal impressions of the soldier that give his work life and colour. Contemporary history in the style of the heroic epic was something entirely new, but established a tradition which lasted to the end of antiquity. Rome's first war with a world power could certainly awaken heroic memories. In his poem Naevius also introduced the founding of Rome and the legend of Dido and Aeneas as origins of the enmity between Rome and Carthage. In this, Vergil, according to his commentators, followed the old poet. Like Livius, Naevius wrote his epic in saturnians.

In detail, much remains problematical, especially the mythological 'pre-history' of the war. Interpretation of the fragments, together with inferences from Vergil, make it very probable that in Naevius's work, as in the first book of the *Aeneid*, the storm, the consoling speech of Aeneas and the conversation between Venus and Jupiter followed one after another ; Anna and Dido also appeared.

The *Bellum Poenicum* did not lose its appeal for a long time ; Cicero compared it to the archaic sculpture of Myron, and Horace tells us that even in his time it was still read. In an epigram on Naevius from the late second century B.C. it is said with some exaggeration that the death of the poet meant the end of Latin speech in Rome.

THE ROMAN THEATRE AND DRAMA

In Naevius the Roman theatre had found its first distinguished playwright. He took over from his predecessor tragedy and comedy in the Greek manner and developed them; the *fabula praetexta* may count as his creation; and if the *fabula togata* cannot be traced back to him with certainty, many of his *palliatae* smoothed the way for it. Tragedy and *praetexta*, *palliata* and *togata* form the 'literary' theatre in the classical period of the Roman Republic; the more improvised dramatic forms, *Atellana* and mime, did not become literary until the next period, the *Atellana* in the time of Sulla, the mime under Caesar.

In the remains of early Roman drama its several forms are very unevenly represented. The *palliata* is known to us directly from the comedies of Plautus and Terence; we can reconstruct at least in general outline a number of tragedies by Ennius and his followers, but the fragments of the *togatae* give at best an idea of its stock themes and its language, and of the *praetexta* not even this can be said. *Praetexta* and *togata* were from the beginning intended as Roman counterparts to the Greek tragedy and comedy; the effect of the *palliata* on the *togata* is beyond dispute, just as later the *togata* in its turn influenced the literary *Atellana*.

This is the place to discuss two problems concerning tragedy and *palliata*: the selection of the Greek originals, and the nature and degree of their transformation. Both are characteristically Roman.

Tragedy leans most heavily on Euripides, the 'most tragic' poet, as Aristotle called him; his rhetorical pathos, and perhaps also his rationalism, made an impression in Rome. In the second place we find Aeschylus, and then the post-classic tragedy. Sophocles, as far as we can see, was less often imitated. He was too 'Attic'. The chorus of classical Greek tragedy was taken over with the plays, but on the Roman stage it became a sort of supernumerary with one speaker; the Roman theatre had no room to offer for the development of a dance accompanying the choral songs. In Seneca the chorus resembles its Greek model, but Seneca's tragedy is a literary product, with no relation to the theatre. The old tragedy of the Romans was rich in lyrical scenes, partly solo, partly divided between several characters.

Most popular were solo scenes in lyric verse without division into stanzas, as found in the late work of Euripides. The Roman tragedians curbed the musical wealth of the Greek choral lyrics; by way of compensation, they gave more room to singing or flute-accompanied recitation (*cantica*), at the expense of the spoken dialogue (*diverbium*). Among forms of lyric verse they evidently preferred those which suited the heavier pace of Latin speech. The Roman public, for whom the themes of Greek tragedy meant but little, apparently demanded, besides more brilliant scenery, more music. This musical element, together with the pathos of language, gives Roman tragedy a strangely baroque character.

The early Attic comedy of Aristophanes and his predecessors, with its mixture of the fantastic and the topical, did not lend itself to being transplanted; even at home it did not survive the Peloponnesian war. Almost all models for the *palliata* belong to the 'new' comedy, whose masters were Menander, Philemon and Diphilos; this is explicitly testified by the prologues and *didascaliae* of the surviving plays. Unfortunately our picture of the new comedy is incomplete, perhaps also one-sided. There are numerous fragments, as the sententiousness of this bourgeois comedy invited quotation; but for this very reason most quotations are not representative of the work as a whole. Menander (died 291 B.C.) is known best. Large parts of five of his comedies were recovered from a papyrus in 1905; now we have also a complete play, *Dyskolos*, 'The Ill-Tempered Man'. This 'new' comedy reflects the muted and slightly sentimental middle-class world of hellenism, whose outlook is confined to private life and its conventional morals; a world ruled by chance, which plays with people, without really meaning harm; it often separates the members of a family and just as unexpectedly unites them again by a chain of strange circumstances (in which signs of recognition play an important role). At the end all turns out well: the courtesan with whom the citizen's son has fallen in love is recognized as a girl of good family, believed lost, and the rebellious slave turns out to be the kidnapped son of his master.

This little world creates character types which comedy appropriates and perfects: the strict or indulgent father, the son who kicks over the traces (but is destined in twenty years' time to have the same trouble with his own son), the seduced girl and her distressed mother, the boastful soldier, the miser, the parasite, the matchmaker, the mother-in-law, the noble courtesan. They never disappeared again from comedy, and were also partly taken over by the sentimental drama. These types can become living people in the hands of a true poet; but even he moves continually in the same world. The author may strive to hold the spectator's attention through a complicated, dexterously constructed plot; but this ingenuity is severely limited by the traditional stock themes, such as the confusion between two characters, exchange of roles, recognition of people missing or believed dead, and that comic situation which depends upon one of the speakers not knowing essential elements of the situation. This picture is, of course, drawn essentially from Menander and his Roman imitators, especially Terence; it is not necessarily true of the new comedy as a whole.

This character comedy was not completely 'Romanized': names and costume establish its characters as Greek, and the action always takes place in a Greek city, usually at Athens. Even the allusions to Roman events and institutions, so familiar in Plautus, do not aim so much at creating a local atmosphere as at dispelling the dramatic illusion and thereby delighting his naïve public. Terence, who modelled himself very strictly on Menander, avoided such things, but he never concealed the fact that he cared only for the approval of an *élite*, the minority of philhellenes. The later *palliata* writers went even farther along this path. This finally estranged the *palliata* from the people and killed it as a living art form.

Destroying the illusion by topical remarks, by asides to the public, by reference to the action as a mere play, etc., was not the only liberty which the Roman poet would take. He would sacrifice the strictly consistent treatment of the plot, he would shorten, lengthen, repeat himself, go off into tirades — anything, if in so doing the action was made more lively and the audience had more occasion to laugh. Again, Terence is the only exception. Sometimes a writer would put into his play a scene from another Greek play. In such a conventional genre as the new comedy, this was often possible without serious harm to the plot. Terence, for example, as he himself said, and Donatus confirmed, had taken elements from Menander's *Perinthia* and put them in his *Andria*. His rival, Luscius Lanuvinus, reproached him for this: *contaminari non decere fabulas* ('it is wrong to spoil the plots'). In defence of this practice Terence invokes the precedent of earlier poets — Naevius, Plautus, Ennius.

Like Roman tragedy, comedy had no real chorus. Even the new comedy of the Greeks knew the chorus only as an *entr'acte*. It did not belong to the play; it was an interlude with which the writer had nothing to do. Common to *palliata* and tragedy is also the distinction of *diverbium* and *cantica*. In Plautus, especially in the later plays, the *cantica* take up a large space. They are mostly solo scenes, 'arias'. Terence is again more restrained: he has far fewer *cantica* than Plautus, and nothing of his metrical wealth.

Besides the drama which came from Greece, there was the theatre which had its roots in folk custom and, at least in its beginnings, was free from foreign influence. The *Atellana* has already been mentioned. Its performers were citizens; they did not have the stigma of the acting profession. The *Atellana* was a farce, in which hoaxing and cheating and obscene ambiguities played a large role. The surviving titles of the later literary *Atellana* emphasize the provincial and rustic; even parody on myths occurred, as in 'Hercules the Tax Collector' (*Hercules Coactor*). The early *Atellana* was probably similar in character. The plays were short and left wide room for improvisation. The actors wore masks and relied on lively gesticula-

tion. The *Atellanae* had stereotyped figures (*personae Oscae*):
Maccus (the clown), Bucco (who constantly had his mouth
open, and thus either 'prattler' or 'moron'), Pappus (the old
man, who was usually duped) and Dossennus (probably the
'hunchback', from a dialect form *dossum* for *dorsum*).

The mime in Rome was part of the festival of Flora on the
28th April. The word 'mime' is Greek; the Greeks, in Greece
as in Italy, knew the mime both as a popular and a literary form
from ancient times. But as far as we can see, the literary mimes
of the Greeks, those of Sophron (fifth century) or Herondas
(third century), had no influence on the Roman mime. The
Roman mime actors wore neither masks nor stage shoes and
were therefore called *planipedes*. Contrary to the general
theatrical convention, women's roles were played by women;
the female 'star' (*archimima*) had her place beside the male one
(*archimimus*). The *mimae*, who appeared heavily painted and
little dressed, were regarded as vulgar. The plays may have
been similar to the *Atellanae*, at any rate when the mime became
literary; again, travesties of myths are found among them.
The mime also had 'stock' characters: the *sannio* ('face-puller')
and the idiot (*stupidus*) with shorn hair.

Details about the theatre do not belong to literary history;
only a few will be mentioned here, which contribute to the
understanding of literary life in Rome. The actors, mostly
foreigners and freedmen, formed regular troupes (*greges*) under
a director (*dominus*), who usually also played the principal role
and was producer. We still know the name of T. Publius Pellio,
who produced two plays of Plautus, and of L. Ambivius Turpio,
the producer of Caecilius Statius and Terence. The actors wore
costume; costume and stage properties were in the charge of a
wardrobe-master (*choragus*). Nothing indicates that each play
was produced with a minimum of actors, as at Athens in the
fifth century. Even allowing for every possibility of doubling
roles, only very few of the surviving plays could be done with
three or four actors, as was the rule in the Attic theatre.

Apart from special occasions (triumphs, funerals of famous men), plays were performed only on state festivals: the *Ludi Megalenses* in honour of the Magna Mater in April (from 204 B.C.), the *Ludi Apollinares* in July (from 212 B.C.), the *Ludi Romani* in September and the *Ludi Plebei* in November, both in honour of Jupiter. As the drama formed part of the religious ceremonies, the officials who had to conduct the games were responsible for it. They hired for the occasion a troupe of actors whose *dominus* acquired the plays from the author (each play was usually produced only once). The theatre, stage and stalls, a crude wooden structure, was erected for the occasion and pulled down again. When in 154 B.C. a stone theatre was first being built, the consul P. Scipio Nasica prohibited the work already in progress and had the senate pass a decree that henceforth not even seats should be erected. This ban lasted for only seven years; but it was not until Pompey that Rome was to have a permanent theatre building. The number of days for performances varied in republican times between eleven and eighteen a year; in the time of Augustus they had grown to forty-three. Actually there were performances far more often, since a way had been found of repeating successful plays. The formality of Roman religion required that a ceremony in which a ritual or technical fault had been made should be wholly or partly repeated. This principle (*instauratio*) could be extended even to a festival lasting several days; nothing more was necessary than to detect or create some irregularity. So we hear that in 205 B.C. and again in 197 B.C. the *Ludi Plebei* had to be celebrated seven times, and it arouses our suspicions that one of the plays of 205 B.C. was the most successful *Miles gloriosus* of Plautus.

The stage was wide, but not deep; it usually represented a street with several houses, which provided entries and exits. The side entrances, according to a none-too-clear convention, were understood to lead to the town centre and the country or seashore respectively; exceptions, as in Plautus's *Rudens*, were

announced as such to the public in the prologue. In the foreground of the stage there stood an altar, where asylum could
be sought in distress. The action took place in the open; even
a banquet was carried on in the street, a convention which for
Southerners was thoroughly plausible. There was no curtain
in early times; the action went on without intervals. The
division of our plays into acts is of later date. The stage conventions were those of the Greek theatre.

The singing and recitation were accompanied on the flute
(*tibia*). There were different types of flute, which were chosen
according to their sound so as to fit the particular character of
the action. The music was specially composed for each play.

The Roman *palliata*, known from the surviving plays of
Plautus and Terence, has shaped the comedy of modern Europe:
Shakespeare and Ben Jonson, Molière and Goldoni grew out of
this tradition. Their types and techniques are still with us:
Oscar Wilde in *The Importance of Being Earnest* revived in a
modern fashion a Plautine plot, and T. S. Eliot's *The Confidential
Clerk* stems directly from Terence.

Q. ENNIUS

Q. ENNIUS is here put before his elder contemporary Plautus
because he was the last universal writer of earlier times. His
work, like that of Naevius, includes epic, tragedy and comedy; he
also introduced didactic poetry, *encomion* and *satura* into Roman
literature. His nephew, Pacuvius, and L. Accius restricted
themselves to tragedy; the latter was also a scholar. Plautus
and his followers were exclusively writers of comedy, Lucilius
a writer of *satura*. Limitation to a single genre became the rule.

Ennius was born in 239 B.C. He came from Rudiae in
Calabria, where Greek, Oscan and Roman influences met.
From an early age he certainly knew, beside the little-known
Messapian, which was his mother tongue, three languages:
Greek, Oscan and Latin. Ennius's years of early manhood fell
in the second Punic war; he served with the Roman auxiliary

troops in Sardinia. There Cato (perhaps as quaestor on his return from Africa in 204 B.C.) got to know him and, impressed by Ennius's personality and talents, took him to Rome. Here Ennius engaged in various activities : he gave lessons in Greek, and successfully adapted Greek plays for the stage. He lived in modest circumstances on the Aventine; perhaps he was attracted to this district by the fact that the guild of writers and actors had its seat there. He soon found his way into the philhellenic circles of high society; among his friends and patrons were men like Scipio Africanus, Scipio Nasica and M. Fulvius Nobilior. The latter took Ennius with him on his Aetolian campaign (189 B.C.), hoping that he would sing the praise of his deeds. In a famous fragment of his *Annals* (Book VII), which introduces a noble Roman and his confidential friend of lower status, Ennius, according to an ancient tradition, portrays his own relationship with Fulvius : a reserved, but intimate, friendship which bridges the gulf between two men from very different spheres of life. When in 184 B.C. Quintus, the son of M. Fulvius, founded a colony, he bestowed civic rights on Ennius as a (nominal) colonist. The poet proudly announces this recognition of his work in the line : *Nos sumus Romani qui fuimus ante Rudini* ('I, who was before a Rudian, am now a Roman'). He died in Rome in 169 B.C., shortly after producing his tragedy *Thyestes* at the Apollinarian games.

Ennius's literary output consists of eighteen books of *Annals*, at least twenty tragedies, two *praetextae*, two *palliatae*, four books of *saturae* and a number of lesser poems. The chronological order of these works is unknown. All that we know for certain is that *Thyestes* falls in the poet's last year; the *Annals* too must have been a work of his old age.

As a dramatist, Ennius preferred tragedy. Most of his tragedies are modelled on Euripides; with his liking for Trojan themes he continues the Roman tradition. For three of his 'Euripidean' tragedies (*Hecuba, Iphigenia, Medea Exsul*) and for his *Eumenides*, modelled on Aeschylus, we still possess the Greek

originals. Comparing these plays with the fragments of their
Latin counterparts, we can watch Ennius at work. Often he
sticks very closely to his model, but just as often he treats it
rather freely, as at the beginning of *Medea* or in Minerva's speech
in the *Eumenides*. His interest in learning is evident in the ety-
mological explanations of Greek names, which he presumably
found in commentaries.

The *praetexta Sabinae* took its material from Roman legend;
in the *Ambracia* Ennius celebrated the conquest of this town
during his patron's Aetolian campaign.

One of his lesser poems, *Sota*, is called after the hellenistic
poet Sotades (third century), who was allegedly shut in a barrel
and thrown into the sea on account of his mocking verses about
the brother-sister marriage of Ptolemaios Philadelphos. The
Scipio, glorifying the deeds of the victor of Zama, must have
been composed soon after the hero's return home, about 201
B.C. Epicharmos is the name of a comic dramatist who worked
in Sicily in the sixth/fifth century B.C. He was credited with
philosophical interests, and later a didactic poem on natural
history went under his name. This seems to have been the basis
of Ennius's *Epicharmus*; he says that he met the poet in a dream
in the underworld, and received his (Pythagorean) wisdom from
his lips. The *Euhemerus* is a translation of the 'sacred histories'
of Euhemeros, who wrote about 403 B.C.: he tells how the gods
were originally mortals, who, on account of their great deeds
and their service to human culture, were raised to divine status.

In the *saturae*, Ennius, though under the influence of hellenism,
created a truly Roman form. The hellenistic interest in Aesop
is seen in the fable of the lark which leaves the field of crops
only when the farmer himself sets about the harvesting. On the
other hand, the allegorical dialogue of Life and Death, which belongs to a widespread type of folk drama, is well rooted in native
tradition. The word *satura* is good Latin, meaning 'stuffing'
or 'medley' (*mélange*), in the double sense of variety of content
and change of metre. Moralizing criticism was in no way

lacking, but as a whole the *saturae* of Ennius were not satirical.

Roman literature also owes to Ennius the epigram in the form of the single elegiac couplet or distich. From Cicero and Seneca we know at least two Ennian epigrams on Scipio, perhaps intended for the front and back of the pedestal of his statue. Cicero also ascribes to Ennius two epigrams on himself; one is an inscription on a portrait, the other his epitaph: *Nemo me lacrimis decoret nec funera fletu / faxit. Cur? Volito vivos per ora virum* ('Let no one honour me with tears, nor weep at my funeral. Why? I am still alive, flying from lip to lip').

Ennius was epoch-making in Latin literature with his historical epic *Annales*. Naevius in his verse chronicle had presented a limited if crucial phase of Roman history, and given a mythological background to the contemporary events in the old legends of Rome and Carthage. Ennius, in a large-scale work of eighteen books, undertook to write the history of Rome from its beginnings to his own time, partly in unpretentious chronicle style, partly in vivid narrative. To the Romans of those times, Rome's ascent to world power was certainly a subject worthy of a poet. Ennius sings of the greatness of Rome; but he gives his message the form and style of the Greek epic. This is his great achievement: to have created an epic which was Greek in its artistic form, Roman in spirit and content. Ennius's goddesses are the Muses of Olympus, not the Camenae of ancient Italy; he himself felt that he was a reincarnation of Homer, the Homer of the Romans, and his poem begins with a dream in which Homer appears and announces to him that his soul, according to the teaching of the Pythagoreans, has entered him, Ennius. He abandons the saturnian as an epic verse; in its place he takes over the Homeric hexameter. Style and language, with their epic epithets and similes, are Homerizing. Homerizing, not Homeric: the Roman is always present, in the religious terms of augural language describing the *augurium* of Romulus and Remus, in a comparison taken from the Roman circus, in such a matter-of-fact line as: *Appius indixit Karthaginiensibus bellum*

('Appius declared war on the men of Carthage'), or *unus homo nobis cunctando restituit rem* ('One man restored the situation for us by delaying'), and generally in the solemn gravity of the language, with its frequent monosyllables at line-endings. This is not just clumsy; it reflects a deliberate attitude of mind.

Ennius worked on the *Annals* right into the last decade of his life; we know, for example, that in the sixteenth book he celebrated the heroic deeds of T. Caecilius Teucer and his brother in the Istrian war of 178/177 B.C. Pliny says that Ennius, impressed by these deeds, continued the *Annals* beyond their original end (fifteenth book), the Aetolian campaign of M. Fulvius Nobilior. The work probably appeared in sections, perhaps in groups of three books (Books 1–3: foundation of Rome and the era of kings; 4–6: early republic to the victory over Pyrrhus; 7–9: war with Carthage).

The title *Annales* is taken from the old city chronicles, the *annales* of the Pontifices, whose year-to-year records were followed by the first historians, Q. Fabius Pictor and L. Cincius Alimentus, at the time of the war with Hannibal. These were also Ennius's most important sources. Like Ennius, they treated the story of Rome's foundation, which had already become traditional.

The *Annals* became the national epic of the Romans and remained so until Vergil composed his *Aeneid*. In the *Aeneid* the epic of Ennius was to be reborn in a new style; Vergil proved his reverence for his great predecessor in those passages where he let the lines of Ennius ring out again and again, and only reverently retouched them.

The *Annals* are the first work of Roman literature of which we have extensive and characteristic fragments, especially through Cicero, who admired Ennius.

COMIC AND TRAGIC DRAMATISTS

T. MACCIUS PLAUTUS — this was probably his full name — was born in Umbrian Sarsina. His year of birth must have fallen some time before 250 B.C. This is implied by Cicero, who says that Plautus wrote the *Pseudolus* (produced in 191 B.C.) as a *senex*, that is, not before the age of sixty. About his life we know next to nothing. He seems to have been an actor in his youth, and the play on his name (Maccus) in the prologue of *Asinaria* is most naturally explained on the assumption that he was the clown (*maccus*) of his troupe. He died in 184 B.C., the year of the censor Cato.

The number of comedies which went under Plautus's name was about 130. Varro, who critically examined their authenticity, believed that apart from the twenty-one which were generally accepted as genuine, a number of others could be attributed to Plautus on stylistic grounds. The rest, says Gellius, included older comedies which Plautus revised (as did Shakespeare in his time) and also plays of one Plautius, who was confused with Plautus. The twenty-one plays attested by Varro have survived (with gaps), but we know the year of production of only two: 200 B.C. for *Stichus* and 191 B.C. for *Pseudolus*.

Plautus devoted himself exclusively to the *palliata*. He took his models almost always from the New Comedy. In *Asinaria* he adapts the 'Donkey-driver' of an otherwise unknown Demophilus, in the 'Casket Comedy' (*Cistellaria*), the 'Breakfasting Women' (*Synaristosai*) of Menander, in *Mercator*, the 'Merchant', and in *Trinummus*, the 'Treasure', of Philemon. The remaining titles of Plautus also have their counterpart in the New (rarely in the Middle) comedy.

Most of the plays are variations on well-known themes. Only the *Amphitruo* is an exception: Jupiter visits Alcmene in the shape of her husband Amphitruo, and Mercury accompanies his divine parent in that of Amphitruo's slave Sosia. The comedy *Menaechmi* is another clever variation on the theme of the 'double'; it involves twin brothers (cf. Shakespeare's *Comedy of Errors*). In *Casina* the young Chalinus and the elderly Olympio woo the same girl. Chalinus plays a trick on his rival :

on the eve of the wedding, dressed as a girl, he goes to Olympio in the place of the expected Casina. Plays like *Captivi*, *Cistellaria* and *Rudens*, whose action culminates in the recognition of a child believed lost, have a more serious background. They are melo-dramas with a sprinkling of comedy. Occasionally the intrigue is very complicated; the understanding of the audience is helped partly by asides, and partly by direct address, but especially by means of prologues which, like those of the later works of Euripides and the New Comedy, outline the action so that the spectator can concentrate entirely on the changing situation. The speaker of the prologue is often either a character of the play (Mercury in *Amphitruo*, Palaestrio in *Miles gloriosus*) or a divine being connected with the plot, but not appearing in the play. Some prologues, however, are not spoken by a dramatic character; in *Captivi*, for example, an actor appears before the public in his own person. Other prologues have been rewritten or are perhaps altogether post-Plautine; this indicates later revivals.

Plautus does not rely primarily on plot; neither does he on character-drawing. The character types after whom many of his plays are called, such as Miles Gloriosus, Mercator, Trucu-lentus, the parasite Curculio ('meal-worm') and the slave Pseudolus ('impudent liar'), had all been created long ago; Plautus made the most of them as he found them, but did not care to differentiate them individually. Most of the figures have names which speak for themselves. This is characteristic of the genre, but Plautus goes one further. Thus in *Miles gloriosus* the stupid, boastful officer is called Pyrgopolynices ('stormer of many towers'); his opposite number in *Pseudolus* is called Polymachaeroplagides, which has two meanings — 'he who deals (or receives) many blows of the sword'.

The irresistible effect of Plautus lies neither in the plot nor in the characters; it comes from his language, whose power, fresh-ness and expressiveness were admired by Varro and Cicero. From the robust swear-words in which he indulges with remarkable gusto to the parody of tragic style, from lyrical mood through the language of passion to an occasional bawdy joke, everything that might at that time come to a Roman's tongue is there, not excluding a little Greek. But the language of Plautus is not realistic; with its accumulated terms of abuse and endearment, its comically monstrous words, its partly exaggerated, partly deliberately incongruous similes, it is the speech of a reality larger than life, much nearer to Aristophanes, whom he did not know, than to Menander and his contemporaries. This language is Roman or, more properly, Italic; with all its exaggeration it is for us a precious source of early Latin, folk-Latin, the language of love and soldiery.

Plautus was the favourite of the Roman public. Even in Cicero's time, when the *palliata* was long since dead, Roscius was able to make a name for himself as an interpreter of Plautus. The Augustans (cf. Hor. *Epist*. II, 1, 170 and following) could make nothing of him; but Probus and the age of Hadrian turned to him again. Plautus was read right to the end of antiquity. The middle ages had on the whole less enthusiasm for Plautus than for the more sententious Terence. Not until the Renaissance was Plautus once more eagerly read; his plays were even performed in schools and universities, and at secular as well as ecclesiastical courts; they have ever since, together with those of Terence, decisively influenced modern comedy.

With CAECILIUS STATIUS, an Insubrian from the region of present-day Milan, Roman comedy begins to adhere more closely to Menander. Caecilius is the first Gaul in Roman literature. Taken prisoner in war, he came to Rome as a slave. After obtaining his freedom he presumably lived on the proceeds of his plays. He shared a house with Ennius; obviously neither of the two was sufficiently well-off to live in a house of his own. Caecilius does not seem to have lived to a great age; he died in 168 B.C., one year after the death of Ennius.

Since Plautus, the writing of comedy had become a specialized job. Like Plautus, Caecilius wrote only *palliatae*. There are approximately forty known titles of his comedies, nearly half of which correspond to titles of Menander; among them are plays with double titles (*e.g.* his *Hypobolimaeus*, 'The Substitute', was also quoted in the Latin form *Subditivus*). Varro praised Caecilius because in his plots he deviates seldom, if ever, from the Greek originals. In details, however, he allows himself as much freedom as does Plautus; this is shown in an instructive comparison of several passages from Caecilius's *Plocium* with Menander's play of the same name by Gellius, who once read both plays one after the other with friends. A narrative in trimeters becomes a lively *canticum*; and in place of the disillusioned reflexions of a faithful slave, we find commonplaces in the bombastic style of tragedy. 'When one reads the Latin play', says Gellius, 'it is very pleasing, but as soon as one compares it with Menander it declines and fades. Instead of the simple humanity and pleasing sincerity of the original, one finds artificiality, and the subtle delineation of character is lost.' Caecilius, says Gellius in conclusion, should not have followed a poet whom he could not reach.

The experiment of approaching more closely Menander's art did not catch on at once; it needed an enterprising director like L. Ambivius Turpio to stage the comedies of Caecilius. Later, Caecilius seems to have won over at least the educated classes; and after the death of Plautus, Caecilius was regarded as the master of Roman comedy. Volcacius Sedigitus, in his catalogue of *palliata* writers, even gives him first place.

P. TERENTIUS AFER was, as his name says, an African. He was called Terentius after the senator Terentius Lucanus, to whose house he came as a slave while still young. His master had him carefully educated and soon gave him his freedom. He died at the age of thirty-five or, according to Suetonius, twenty-five. What we are told about Terence's private life deserves little credence. We are better informed about his career as a dramatist. Besides the *didascaliae* of his comedies we have the prologues of the plays themselves, in which Terence answers his critics. Firstly, we know the dates of the production of six comedies: *Andria* (166 B.C.), the first production of *Hecyra* ('The Mother-in-Law', 165 B.C.), *Heautontimorumenos* ('The Self-Tormentor', 163 B.C.), *Eunuchus* and *Phormio* (161 B.C.), *Adelphoe* and a second production of *Hecyra* at the funeral games for Aemilius Paulus (160 B.C.), and a third production of *Hecyra* at the *Ludi Romani* of the same year. Soon afterwards Terence embarked for Greece, from where he was not to return; he died in 159 B.C. He left a country estate to his daughter, who later married a Roman knight.

That *Hecyra* was staged three times within a few years was caused by the fact that twice it proved a failure: the first production was broken off because the public was already impatient to see a boxing match and a rope-dancer; during the second production a rumour spread among the spectators that there were to be gladiatorial games, and they flocked to the stronger attraction; only the third production, which had no similar rival, brought success. The aediles who accepted the unsuccessful play had confidence in its value, but it seems to have found a public only for lack of better entertainment. This is understandable: *Hecyra* is poor in action and its refined conversational tone demands greater attention than was to be expected of Roman theatregoers in Terence's time.

If Terence was not very popular with the general public, neither was he 'pure' enough for the literary critics. A little known older poet who bore him a grievance (Luscius Lanuvinus, as Donatus tells us) had accused him of 'contamination', plagiarism, and even outside assistance. The criticism of contamination was levelled against *Andria*, which contained elements of Menander's *Perinthia*. Terence referred to the practice of Naevius, Plautus and Ennius and pleaded his particular case with the similarity of the two plots. The charge of plagiarism (here the adaptation of a Greek comedy which had already been put on the stage by a previous playwright) was brought against

Eunuchus and *Adelphoe*.   Of *Eunuchus* it was said that Terence
had introduced a character from the 'Flatterer' of Menander,
and in *Adelphoe* a scene (kidnapping of a girl from a brothel)
came from Diphilos's *Synapothneskontes* ('Together Until
Death').   Terence admits both, but does not regard himself as
guilty.   He declares he had no knowledge of the *Colax* ('Flatterer') of Plautus, which at a time when comedies circulated
only in stage-copies was quite possible, and the scene from
Diphilos had been passed over by Plautus so that it was still 'free'.
In the prologue to *Phormio*, Terence answers Luscius on a criticism of his work as a whole ; he even attacks his critic and advises
him to take a critical view of himself.   Luscius, who had put on
the stage, among other plays, Menander's 'Apparition' and
'Treasure', had translated them so literally that he was incom-
prehensible to the ordinary Roman.   Of an unnamed comedy of
Luscius, Terence says (*Phormio*, prol. 10) that it owed its success
mainly to the acting.   Terence's judgement of Luscius is confirmed by Sedigitus, who places him second last in his list of
comic poets.   Perhaps the calumnious Luscius (*Heautont.*, prol.
22) was guildmaster of the *collegium* of poets ; rather unsuccessful
himself, he may have hoped to prevent Terence's rise to fame by
his criticism.

Far from being a slavish imitator of Menander, Terence, like
Caecilius, only in a more subtle (and therefore less effective) way,
endeavoured to preserve his independence as an artist.   He did,
however, accept the challenge of Menander's greatness : his
own creation was to breathe the spirit of Menander's art.   After
the last production of *Hecyra* he went to Greece, to get to know
Greek life from personal experience, perhaps even in the hope
of discovering comedies of Menander which were still unknown
in Rome.   However, he died in the following year.

The ancients knew only the six comedies by Terence which
we still have.   Valerius Probus published them in a critical
edition ; this is the basis of our Terence text.

Two comedies of Terence are adapted from Apollodoros of

Karystos, of whom we know little, the remaining four from Menander. Differences between the 'Apollodoros plays' and the 'Menander plays' are noticeable only in the construction of their plots and therefore belong to the originals; *e.g.* Apollodoros exposes the plot through slaves, who discuss their masters (this technique had not yet died out), while Menander prefers exposition through a principal character who at the same time reveals his own nature. Some of Menander's comedies, however, begin with a slave dialogue, *e.g.* the *Arbitration*, in which the slave Onesimos answers the inquisitive questions of a cook about his master. After the short opening dialogue there usually follows a prologue, spoken by a god, which contains the essential part of the exposition. Terence, however, prefers the exposition in dialogue to the exposition in monologue.

From Menander, Terence also learned the art of indirect characterization through speech, on which Donatus so lucidly comments. But Terence's style is his own achievement. He substitutes for the Attic colloquial language the conversational Latin of a cultured Roman society refined by their contact with the Greeks. One is inclined to think that Terence might not have caught the finest shades of tone without his noble friends, and so the reproach that he availed himself of their collaboration contains perhaps a grain of truth. (Joseph Conrad wrote under the eyes of George Moore, and Evelyn Waugh had expert advice on the Americanisms in 'The Loved One' from competent quarters.)

The purity of Terence's language is praised by Cicero. More reserved in his appreciation is Caesar, who parodies Cicero's praise. Caesar admits the poet's purity and polish of language, but misses in him Menander's comic force.

If Terence deliberately adopted Menander's plots and characters and his art of characterization by speech, he also absorbed in his work some of Menander's mellow philosophy of life. The time was ripe for it. The old *virtus* had not been abandoned, but the harshness with which it was once practised was on the

decline. Officially there was no place in Rome for the free and
easy ways of the Athenians; the *palliata* with its prodigals and
courtesans, with seductions and adultery, has Athens as its scene.
But a readiness to understand, a reflecting and tolerant frame of
mind, seems, within certain limits, to have developed with the
growing influence of Greek culture and the refined ways of
private and social life. It is characteristic that Terence twice, in
Heautontimorumenos and even more expressly in *Adelphoe*, takes
up the question of how to bring up one's children and that the
ancestral severity in both cases achieves the opposite of what it
aims at. *Homo sum: humani nihil a me alienum puto* ('I am a
human being: I think nothing human to be foreign to me'),
says Chremes in *Heautontimorumenos* (l. 25). The line ex-
presses a sentiment for which the Romans coined the word
humanitas.

Next we turn to tragedy. M. PACUVIUS, for Cicero the
greatest among the Roman tragedians, lived from the years of
Plautus's manhood to the time of the Gracchi. He was born in
Brundisium in about 220 B.C. Ennius, whose nephew he was,
took him to Rome, where he painted and wrote tragedies.
Pacuvius lived to a ripe old age. The production of one of his
plays is attested for as late as 140 B.C., when he was an octogen-
arian; then he retired to Tarentum for the sake of his health,
and died there about 130 B.C.

Pacuvius was not a prolific writer. The five hundred odd
lines that have survived are from no more than thirteen plays:
twelve tragedies and one *praetexta*. As a poet Pacuvius went
his own way. He preferred out-of-the-way and little-known
themes, such as the post-Euripidean tragedy would offer him.
Among the titles are *Dulorestes* ('Orestes the Slave' — the
avenger Orestes in this play would seem to have gone back to
Mycenae disguised as a slave), *Iliona* and *Niptra*. The *praetexta*
Paulus probably celebrated the victory of L. Aemilius Paulus at
Pydna, 168 B.C.

Pacuvius gave even more space in his tragedies to philosophical speculation than did Ennius; Horace calls him *doctus*
(*Epist*. II, 1, 36). His language has power and fullness (*ubertas*,
says Varro); the thrilling description of a thunderstorm at sea
gives a good idea of it. Cicero, however, says Pacuvius lacked
linguistic purity. An author who strives for expressiveness is
seldom a purist. His description of the dolphins as *Nerei repandi-
rostrum incuruiceruicum pecus* ('Nereus's animals with upturned
snouts and curving necks') was parodied first by Lucilius, and
Quintilian quoted the line as a warning example of monstrous
word formation.

One might think that Pacuvius's work was not very popular.
But according to all we know his tragedies were a great success
on the stage; they were performed even after his death and were
read for a long time. We can now appreciate only the grandeur
of isolated passages; none of the plays can be reconstructed
despite the numerous fragments. Pacuvius must have impressed
his audience partly by the intensity of his dramatic situations,
partly by his power of words, which carried the spectator away
even if he did not understand everything.

Linguistic power coupled with greater linguistic discipline
characterized the younger contemporary of Pacuvius, the
tragedian L. ACCIUS. Horace (*Epist*. II, 1, 56) gives him the
epithet *altus* ('the sublime'). Accius, too, produced a tragedy
in Rome in 140 B.C. He had been born as the son of a freedman
at Pisaurum in 170 B.C.; the young Cicero still knew him
personally.

In contrast to Pacuvius, Accius was extremely prolific; we
know no less than forty-five of his tragedies and two *praetextae*
(*Brutus* and *Aeneadae* — the latter had the self-sacrifice of the
younger P. Decius Mus, 295 B.C., for its subject). In the choice
of his models, among which Euripides is much represented, and
in his liking for Trojan themes, he harks back to the old Roman
tragedy; yet he treated his material with great freedom. A

saying of his tyrannical Atreus: *Oderint, dum metuant* ('Let them hate, as long as they fear'), has remained alive until today.

The esteem which Accius enjoyed is demonstrated by his position in the *Collegium scribarum*; conscious of his own greatness as a writer, he never rose from his seat when an upper-class amateur, C. Iulius Caesar Strabo, came to the meetings.

THE BEGINNINGS OF PROSE

Poenico bello secundo Musa pinnato gradu | intulit se bellicosam in Romuli gentem feram ('In the second Punic war, the Muse with winged step came to the fierce and warlike people of Romulus'). With these words, whose rhythm has certainly much more of the tread of the legions than of the 'winged step' of the muse, Porcius Licinus a hundred years later sings of the birth of Roman poetry, which had its first flowering at the time of the war with Hannibal. In the years of the war with Hannibal also fall the beginnings of Roman prose.

Curiously, while the Greek Andronicus and the Messapian Ennius were pioneers of poetry in the Latin language, Rome's earliest historians — men belonging to old families and of senatorial rank — wrote Greek. Certainly, Greek was the civilized language in the Mediterranean, from Alexandria and Corinth to Massilia and Carthage. It is understandable that the Roman of the times began to see his own past in a world-wide historical context, and that he wanted to tell his history to that world in its own language. Rome had become too important to be put on a level with the rest of the barbarians, even by the culturally proud Greeks. And yet to impress the cultured Greek world was hardly their sole motive. Basically these distinguished Romans wrote for Romans.

We call these first historians of Rome the earlier annalists; the original titles of their works no longer remain, but Cicero, and later Livy, speak of *Graeci annales* and *prisci annales*. The later Latin translations of the historical work of Q. Fabius Pictor and C. Acilius were doubtless called *Annales*. The terminological difference beween *historiae* (contemporary history) and *annales* (history of the past) best known, from Tacitus, belongs to a later time.

The earliest annalists began with the foundation of the city and carried its story down to their own day. Despite the annalistic style the presentation was in no way so dull as the annals of the *pontifices*. The Greek historian shaped his material as an artist, and the Romans, in this as in other things, emulated the Greeks. Acilius went so far as to invent a meeting of Hannibal and Scipio in Ephesos, in order to confront the great generals in the flesh instead of merely comparing them in retrospect; we now concede such freedom only to the poet.

The earliest of the annalists is Q. FABIUS PICTOR. His lifetime is approximately determined by the fact that after the defeat of Cannae (216 B.C.) he was appointed leader of a legation to the Delphic oracle. He began his story with the foundation of Rome (dated 747 B.C.), including its 'prehistory', and continued it to his own time. He wrote at length, and with a sprinkling of rhetoric. Polybius, who drew on him for his history of the Punic wars, acknowledged his veracity, which was only occasionally spoilt by patriotic prejudice. He also seems to have put the merits of the Fabian family, to which he belonged, very much in the foreground, and to have been prejudiced against the Claudians, of whom the Fabians were enemies.

L. CINCIUS[1] ALIMENTUS, from a plebeian family, was somewhat younger than Fabius. He was praetor in 210 B.C.; in the following year he was sent to Sicily with the difficult task of commanding the remainder of the army beaten at Cannae, and restoring their discipline. Later he fell into the hands of Hannibal, who treated him with respect and conversed with

[1] He should not be confused with another L. Cincius, who was an antiquarian, and perhaps a contemporary of Cicero.

him on military matters. Cincius's historical work also began
with Rome's 'prehistory' and ended with the latest events.

A. POSTUMIUS ALBINUS (cos. 151 B.C.) belongs to a later
generation; he was a younger contemporary of Cato, whose
scorn he attracted by his pronounced philhellenism. Apart
from his annals, Albinus seems to have treated the Aeneas legend
in a separate work.

C. ACILIUS, a contemporary of Albinus, functioned as interpreter in proceedings of the senate with a legation of Athenian
philosophers in 155 B.C. In his historical writing he seems to
have been fond of telling anecdotes; one of the few fragments
tells how a Roman prisoner of war, discharged under oath for
the purpose of getting back some captive Carthaginians, returned under the pretext of having forgotten something, was
once more discharged — unconditionally — and so, without
fulfilling his mission, stayed at Rome for good. We have here
the negative counterpart of the Regulus legend.

The son of the elder Scipio also wrote a historical work in
Greek. L. Cassius Hemina (about 146 B.C.) and his contemporary, Cn. Gellius, were the first to break away from Greek;
the historians of the Gracchian era wrote in Latin.

Juridical writing served purely practical purposes. The first
important work of Roman jurisprudence came to be written at
the beginning of the second century B.C.: the *Tripertita* of Sex.
Aelius Paetus (cos. 198 B.C.). This collection contained not only
the text of the Twelve Tables and the *legis actiones*, but also legal
interpretation (*interpretatio*), for which a tradition had already
developed from numerous legal decisions (*responsa*). This *Ius
Aelianum* was known to later jurists as the 'cradle of Roman Law'.

Much older than the written word is the spoken word.
Formal speech was no less at home in the Roman republic than

in the Greek city states. The practice of law and such institutions of public life as senate meetings and popular assemblies developed those types of speech which in the rhetorical schools came to be called *controversiae* and *suasoriae*, and from the old custom of the funeral speech grew the *laudatio* — those three categories of the art of oratory which the Greeks had long since developed from a similar background and had formalized in their rhetoric. Until the second century Rome knew neither a theory of oratory nor a systematic education of the orator; Romans relied either on natural talent or on tradition and practice. The Italian temperament gave the speech of the Roman verve and liveliness, and his *gravitas* lent it dignity. The style of the great orators of Greece and the manner of their hellenistic followers, however, was hardly without influence even in the third century; and with the closer connexion of Rome with Greek culture, this influence steadily increased. But the time had not yet come when Greek rhetoricians introduced Roman youth to the casuistry of Hermagoras, and when budding orators went to Athens and Rhodes to perfect their art.

A speech is not a work of literature unless it is published. At first this would have happened but rarely. If Appius Claudius, as is probable, published his speech against the peace with Pyrrhus, he did so as a manifesto of his policy. Nothing similar is known from the great times of the Punic wars, although there was then no lack of remarkable orators. The eloquence of M. Cornelius Cethegus (cos. 204 B.C.) was commemorated by Ennius, who had heard him, yet his speeches were not published. Cicero read the funeral oration of Fabius Cunctator at the death of his son and admired the speaker's philosophical composure; but the text would have been kept in the family archives, and might have been published at some later date.

The first who made it a rule to publish his orations was M. PORCIUS CATO. He came from a plebeian family of Latin

Tusculum, where he was born in 234 B.C. His youth was spent on the family estate in Sabine Reate. He entered politics as a *novus homo*, the first of his family to run for high offices. As a young man he distinguished himself in several campaigns of the second Punic war, lastly in the battle at Sena (207 B.C.). As consul (195 B.C.) he triumphed over the Spaniards and as an officer of M.' Acilius Glabrio he decided the battle of Thermopylae against Antiochus (191 B.C.). In his provincial administraion he was harsh yet incorruptible; he defended Sardinia against the Roman profiteers. He met the hellenized upper classes with open hostility; this was evident as early as his quaestorship (205 B.C.). We know that Cato later led political attacks against the Scipios, and reproached Fulvius Nobilior in a speech for taking poets (of course Ennius is meant) with him into his province (Cic. *Tusc.* I, 3). Also in his proverbial censorship (184 B.C.), he not only opposed extravagance and luxury, but also took the opportunity to purge the senate of elements which he thought undesirable. He was a man of tenacious will-power, who never lost sight of an aim once conceived; most famous is his persistent *Delenda est Carthago*, which he never tired of repeating since he had personally convinced himself (152 B.C.) of the renewed prosperity of that city. He lived to see the declaration of war, but not the destruction of the rival; he died at the end of 149 B.C.

That a man like Cato should have adversaries, if not outright enemies, was inevitable. But he was never defeated. Forty times he stood trial, and was always acquitted. He owed this undoubtedly to his strong personality, of which every word of his gave evidence. In his speech he combined a peasant's shrewdness and mother-wit with the rhetorical technique of the Greeks, which he used without finesse, but all the more effectively. Attack seemed to him the best defence; even Cicero, who worshipped him, recognized that invective was one of his most outstanding characteristics. Cato saw to it that his word was not forgotten. He published all his orations, the political as well

as the legal ones. Cicero gives the number of Cato's speeches
known to him as more than one hundred and fifty. We still
know some eighty of them from fragments. We have a fairly
clear picture of some orations, *e.g.* of his defence of the Rhodians
(167 B.C.). The fragments confirm Cicero's opinion: he praises
Cato's prose for its wealth of thought, clear construction, gravity,
power and liveliness, and takes the lack of elegance and smoothness as an archaic imperfection. We may well believe Cicero
that no Roman orator before Cato was worth reading.

In publishing his orations, Cato only made a rule of what had
been done occasionally before him. He did something entirely
new when he wrote his *Origines* in the Latin language. He
deliberately broke away from both the dry city chronicles and
the hellenized annals of Fabius and his followers. His theme is
not 'Rome and the Greek World' but 'Rome and Italy'. After
he had treated the history of Rome from her foundation to the
fall of the kings in the first book, he treated in books 2 and 3 the
origins (*origines*) of the Italian towns, over which Rome gradually
extended her dominion. With book 4 began the first Punic
war. Book 5 contained the second war, books 6 and 7 contem,
porary history almost to Cato's death. In all Roman literature,
nothing is comparable to Cato's *Origines*. And yet even this
work could not have been conceived without the Greeks. A
comparison with Herodotus is suggested even by its construction; before Cato's time and in his own day, Greeks, extending
their interests to the West, had written foundation histories of
Italian towns. For all that, the *Origines* are a highly individual
work. Having reproached the annalists for the glorification of
their own families, Cato on principle suppresses the names
of Rome's generals; even the heroic deed of the tribune
Q. Caedicius in the first Punic war was told without giving the
hero's name; the only name recorded is that of the brave
elephant Surus in the Carthaginian army. True to his principle-
Cato himself remained anonymous in his work. This did not
prevent him, however, from giving himself credit where he

thought it was due. He even inserted the complete text of some
of his speeches.

With the *Origines*, Cato wanted to set up a national historiography against that of the hellenizing annalists; with his writings
on agriculture, hygiene and the art of oratory, he challenged the
encyclopaedic works of the Greeks. He chose the conventional
Roman form of instruction to his own son: *Orator est, Marce
fili, vir bonus dicendi peritus . . . , Agricola vir bonus, Marce fili,
colendi peritus. . . .* The style is terse, as in the old laws: *Rem
tene, verba sequentur* ('hold fast to your subject, the words will
follow'). Cato also wrote on law and warfare and (in prose)
composed a *Carmen de moribus*, in which he — not the first and
not the last — complains about the bad times and the decay of
morals.

(The so-called *Monosticha* and *Disticha Catonis* — the latter
not elegiac but hexametric couplets — date from the later empire.
Despite their patent opportunism they were much read in the
Christian middle ages and in the early Renaissance, often translated and adapted and popularly used as a school-book; even
today the primer is called *catón* in Spanish.)

Cato's attitude to the Greek world is full of contradictions, as
is his whole personality. Behind the patriarchal Roman of the
old type stands a man who is deeply impressed by the power of
Greek culture, and even more deeply disturbed. He was convinced that the Greek doctors with their expensive art would
only sap the Romans' strength; he also saw in Greek intellec-
tuality a danger to his ideals of courageous practical action. That
is why he insisted that the Athenian philosophers who had come
to Rome (156/155 B.C.) as ambassadors, and had begun to attract
Roman youth by their teaching, should leave as soon as their
mission was completed. The scepticism of Carneades in particular, the founder of the New Academy, who was a member of
the legation, must have aroused his suspicion. He could never
help feeling that the Greek only looked down on the Roman who
tried to be like him. Yet he saw clearly that the fact of Greek

intellectual superiority had to be honestly faced; in his old age
he even devoted himself to the study of Greek. He tried to meet
the enemy on his own ground. In this way Cato came to be the
founder of Latin prose. Inevitably he was in some degree
affected by the forces which he fought. The summary rejection
of all things Greek in his commands to his son has something of
over-compensation. As an old man he consented to the marriage
of his son to the sister of the philhellene Scipio.

Of Cato's vast literary output a single work has survived complete: *De agri cultura*. It is not the compendium which he
composed for his son, but a guide for farmers, in simple language,
based to some extent on Greek agricultural literature, but above
all on his own experience.

Its diverse contents can only be briefly indicated. There we
read about practically everything that concerns life on a country
estate: we not only hear about work on the land, from dung-
spreading to oil-pressing, but also of sacrifices and prayers, of
spells and medicines, of housework and cooking recipes. Again
and again strict economy is insisted on: the slaves' food, drink
and clothing are severely rationed, and whoever gets a new
garment must give up the old one as the rags are still good for
patching; bad weather must be used for work in the house and
yard; equipment for livestock and fields is to be carefully looked
after, but the old or ailing slave must be sold. The steward
(*vilicus*) is responsible to his master for management and produce,
and should be regularly checked and held to accurate rendering
of accounts. He must understand agricultural work, otherwise
he has no authority; he is expected to lend a hand occasionally,
but not too often, for he has other things to do. His wife
(*vilica*), whom his master chooses for him, must rarely go out,
not often invite in neighbours or be invited by them, keep the
house in order and look up to her husband. Prudence must be
the rule in buying property. A glance at the neighbours is no
less important than the position of the site and the condition of the
soil. The estate must produce surplus for the market; here, as

in the writings to Marcus, economy in matters great and small is represented as vital: *Patrem familias vendacem non emacem esse oportet* ('The father of the house should be selling, not buying'). Produce from agriculture, it is said right at the beginning, is the best and most worthy way of money-making. Trade yields more, but has greater risks; banking is even more profitable but not respectable. Here speaks the senator, to whom trade, not to mention money-lending, were forbidden by law.

This little book is not great literature. But its Italic style, which is preserved even in spite of the modernization in which we read it, and the lively picture of Italian farming in the second century B.C. which it draws, make it a precious testimony of the Roman way of life. Here the real Cato stands before us: circumspect, provident, economical, strict to the point of harshness 'and more concerned about his cattle than about his slaves; unsentimental in the running of his estate as he was in politics; no philanthropist, but a man of common sense, and one in a long line of generations who shaped the Italian country-side.

THE 'FABULA TOGATA'

The *fabula togata*, comedy in Roman costume, may partly be understood as a reaction against hellenism. According to a note attributed to Donatus, which we cannot verify, the *fabula togata* was 'invented' by Livius Andronicus. In Naevius and still more in Plautus the Italian temperament and Roman local colour are unmistakable, yet they did not create a new form of drama. Only when, with Caecilius and Terence, the *palliata* was more and more thoroughly hellenized, and when, perhaps, the stock of Greek plays was becoming exhausted and themes, situations and characters were being used up, did the desire for a 'Roman' comedy take shape; it is symptomatic that this innovation, as far as we can see, falls in the later years of Cato's life.

Of the writers of *togatae* we know three by name: Titinius, L. Afranius and T. Quinctius Atta. The last-mentioned died in

77 B.C., Titinius might have been an older contemporary of
Terence, and Afranius probably belongs in the later second
century. About the lives of these poets we know absolutely
nothing. The approximately seventy titles and six hundred and
fifty lines which have come down to us give a general impression
of themes and characters and just allow us to recognize Titinius
and Afranius as individual artists.

The action of the *togata* takes place in Italy; sometimes in
Rome, sometimes in the country. Its characters are Romans
or Italians, but (in contrast to the *praetexta*) people of the lower
classes; for this reason the *togata* is also called *tabernaria*, the
comedy of the small shopkeepers and wine-sellers. The action
is freely invented but generally takes its themes and situations,
as the fragments show, from Greek comedy and its Roman
equivalent. Unfortunately few plays, if any, can be even
approximately reconstructed. Characteristic of the native *milieu*
is the big role played by women and the fact that slaves were not
drawn as cleverer than their masters. The spoken line is that of
the *palliata*, but lyrical metres are rare.

If more of the *togata* had survived, we would have a comprehensive picture of the life of small people in town and country in
the Italy of the second century B.C. Even the titles are revealing: they refer to small craftsmen and business people, weavers,
hair dressers and innkeepers; to festivals like the *Compitalia*, the
feast of the rural Lares, which were worshipped at cross-roads (*com-
pita*); and to other occasions which might provide excitement,
such as auctions, crimes and lawsuits. The *togata* too has its types,
but they are not those of the *palliata*: *Prodigus* (the spendthrift),
Temerarius (the daredevil), *Simulator* (the malingerer), even the
female amateur lawyer (*Iurisperita*). Many of its favourite
themes are taken from home life: family and relations, servants
and neighbours, the son who is dismissed from his father's control
(*Emancipatus*), the freedman (*Libertus*), sisters (*Sorores*), cousins
(*Consobrini*), aunts (*Materterae*), stepson (*Privignus*), sisters-in-law
(*Fratriae*); of course there are also the enemy neighbours

(*Inimici*).   In the same sphere belong love and marriage affairs :
the eloping girl (*Abducta*), the love-letter (*Epistula*), the rejected
suitor (*Repudiatus*).   The contrast of province and capital (also
a timeless source of comedy) is suggested by such titles as *Setina*,
Veliterna, *Brundisinae*, which are named after Italian towns.

The *togata* had its purest representative in Titinius.   Even in
his titles, the provincial and rustic element predominates.   His
language too was rustic ; he is much quoted by Nonius for the
sake of his archaisms.   The fragments have something Plautine
about them, but one need not on this account place him near
Plautus in time ; he may well, in deliberate opposition to the
followers of Menander, have fallen back on the earthiness of the
earlier comedy.   Afranius, on the other hand, was an admirer of
Terence, and his *togatae* show Terence's influence ; in his work
character-types and family themes prevail and his idiom is purer
and smoother.   He turns the *togata* into a petit-bourgeois drama.
It did not outlive the time of Sulla, but there were occasional
later revivals.   The many-sided C. Melissus towards the end of
the reign of Augustus made an attempt to raise it to a higher
social level in the form of the *trabeata*, the 'knights' comedy'
(*trabea* was the name of the formal dress of the Roman knight).
The knights, for a long time the 'financial nobility' of Rome,
were one of the privileged classes of the new regime.   This gave
the experiment topicality but not duration : the *trabeata* died
with its creator.

THE SCIPIONIC CIRCLE AND THE ROMAN WORLD OF THEIR TIME

When Cicero, in the late days of the republic, wrote his work
On the State, he gave it the form of a dialogue between Roman
statesmen on the best form of government.   He laid the scene of
these conversations on the estate of the younger Scipio at the
feriae Latinae of the year 129 B.C.   There we meet Scipio himself,
his nephew Q. Aelius Tubero, L. Furius Philus, the lawyer M.'
Manilius, C. Laelius and his two sons-in-law C. Fannius and

C

Q. Mucius Scaevola, Sp. Mummius and the young P. Rutilius
Rufus; mention is made also of the philosopher Panaetius,
the historian Polybius and the astronomer C. Sulpicius Gallus.
Rufus, who, as an old man, was visited by Cicero in 78 B.C., is
made his authority for what he allegedly reports.

Cicero, in imitation of Plato, gave his philosophical dialogue
a historical setting; he deliberately chose a moment when the
Roman state was still at its height, and assembled a group of men
who, in the shadow of a danger threatening from within, might
well reflect on the spiritual and moral foundations of their own
form of life and government. In these men of distinction,
culture and personality, Cicero saw the realization of everything
that he himself most treasured; he would find comfort in looking
back from the chaos of his own time to that world from which
he was separated by only two generations, and with which he
had personal contacts through such men as P. Rutilius Rufus
and Q. Mucius Scaevola. But in Cicero's nostalgia this
world becomes idealized; we must never forget this when
speaking of the Scipio circle. Its spirit lives for us as it lived in
Cicero.

In the four decades from the triumph of Paulus over Perseus
(168 B.C.) to the death of the younger Scipio (129 B.C.) Rome
had politically and spiritually reached its zenith, in the double
sense of a climax and a turning point. The successor states to
the Kingdom of Alexander had one after the other come under
Roman rule; under the will of King Attalus III in 133 B.C. the
Pergamenian Kingdom also fell to the Romans; only Egypt
preserved a more nominal than real independence. As the power
of Rome increased, so did her wealth: since the gigantic booty
from Pydna the Roman citizen was no longer required to pay
taxes; with the destruction of Carthage and Corinth in 146 B.C.
Rome assumed undisputed control of the entire Mediterranean
market; the heritage of Attalus made one of the richest and most
civilized countries of the East a Roman province. With wealth
came luxury and corruption, the latter especially in provincial

administration where the temptation was greatest, and soon also in politics. The brunt of it was borne by the Italian peasant. Through the collapse of the smaller farms (due to prolonged service in the wars) and the competition of the large landowners, who established plantations on the Carthaginian pattern, the peasantry had become more and more impoverished and involved in debt; often a farmer had to sell his property and move into town where the growing proletariat became a dangerous weapon of political parties or ambitious individuals.

From this background with its lights and shadows there stands out a group of men to whom the power and wealth which they had won for Rome were a means of transplanting Greek culture to their native state. The conquerors of the hellenistic Kingdoms were all philhellenes, from Flamininus, the victor of Cynoscephalae, to L. Mummius, the destroyer of Corinth. (The cultural aspirations of the latter, however, were more enthusiastic than enlightened. He is said to have threatened a crew who had to ship masterpieces of Greek art from Corinth to Italy: 'If you let these things drown, you will have to remake every one of them').

To speak and write Greek had long since become a matter of course for the cultured. Negotiations were carried on with the Greeks in their own language (only Cato insisted on an interpreter), decrees of the senate affecting the East were issued in Greek, and the father of the Gracchi made a speech in Greek on the island of Rhodes in 164 B.C. Even the writers of comedy could expect their public to have some knowledge of Greek, and this was true not only of the *élite* for whom Terence wrote, but also of the much wider public of Plautus.

The Roman philhellenes were not content to read Greek poetry in Latin translation or adaptation: they read the Greeks in the original. Nothing characterizes a man like L. Aemilius Paulus better than that he took nothing from the booty of Pydna for himself except the royal library, from which his sons could satisfy their thirst for education. Until then the Romans had been impressed above all by Greek poetry; now they began to realize more and more the cultural value of historiography, and of something entirely new to Rome: philosophy.

Not that Rome had hitherto remained untouched by philosophical ideas. The poem of Appius Claudius was, according to Cicero, 'Pythagorean': Pythagorean ideas might easily have spread from the colonies of Southern Italy. Neither is Menander untouched by philosophy; his wisdom is the heritage of a century which had learnt from Socrates to think about the spiritual and ethical nature of man and his place in the world. Yet the little of Greek philosophy that reached Rome by such indirect ways was assimilated only in the form of practical maxims. For a long time Romans would distrust Greek philosophy as much as they distrusted the Greek mystery cults. In 186 B.C. the senate, with drastic measures, repressed the Dionysian cult in Italy; in 173 B.C. two Epicurean philosophers were expelled; in 161 B.C. there followed a general decree of expulsion against all philosophers and rhetoricians, and in 155 B.C. Cato saw to it that the Athenian philosophers (Carneades, Critolaos and Diogenes), who had come on an official mission, left the city again as soon as possible. But in the long run such measures had no effect. Things would take a different turn as soon as the right people on either side came into contact.

The decisive event took place in the house of L. Aemilius Paulus. In 167 B.C. a thousand distinguished Achaeans were taken to Italy as hostages. Among them was the educated POLYBIUS, who had played a role in the politics of the Achaean League. While the majority of these hostages were confined for sixteen years to Italian towns, Polybius had the good fortune to come to the house of Paulus. The general made him tutor of his sons. Polybius won the affection of the young Publius, and became his permanent companion. Deeply impressed by the greatness of Rome and Roman ways, he made himself the herald of Rome's mission in a historical work, which according to the original plan was to be concluded with the victory of

Paulus over Perseus. He saw in Rome's world power not so much the work of fate as the result of Roman ability, and explained Rome's success by the Roman constitution, which he understood as a harmonious balance of the three basic forms of government; monarchy, aristocracy and democracy.

Of no less influence was PANAETIUS from Rhodes, who taught a moderate stoicism. He too belonged to the entourage of Scipio, whom he accompanied on a diplomatic journey to the East and to Alexandria. The practical philosopher and the philosophizing historian Polybius got to know one another through Scipio.

The belief in Rome's historical mission and an exacting code of personal ethics, both deriving from stoicism, came to be integrated, for the Roman, in his devotion to the state. The traditional ethics (*mos maiorum*) were now understood as the special Roman form of a general law. It was crystallized in the concept of *virtus*, which is rather more comprehensive and at the same time more specific than 'virtue' : it means something like 'the qualities of a true man' (*vir*).

But *virtus* alone was no longer sufficient. It was embedded, one might almost say absorbed, in the concept of *humanitas*. Both are ideals of life and so elude a strict definition; but *humanitas* is even more difficult to describe, because it is something much more complex. Tentatively, *humanitas* is the entire 'human-ness' of the individual in all his concrete social relations. It begins with a well-groomed appearance and gracious living — dress, dwelling, household effects — which keeps the exact balance between shabbiness and luxury. It includes the enjoyment of beauty in nature and art; an appreciation of the mind's world as something specifically human; respect of one's fellow beings and a sympathetic interest in all that affects them; a feeling for what is consistent with the nature of man (not unlike the Greek philosophical idea of 'life in accordance with nature') ; a ready acceptance of one's obligations towards gods and men — *religio*, *pietas*, *virtus*, displayed towards the individual as towards the state. This general attitude manifests itself no less in pleasing manners and a cultured way of speech, which combines dignity with charm, than in something as comprehensive as international law (*ius gentium*), in which the stoic idea of *koinonia*, the 'human community', takes a tangible form.

Was the gulf between Scipio and Cato really so great? The fragments of Scipio's orations show the same respect for tradition, manly discipline, determined opposition to luxury and decadence. Only the centre of gravity has shifted: the old morality is no longer a command that must be obeyed blindly, but a law the meaning of which is understood. In a similar way Scipio's more supple style, which when necessary is not lacking in force, contrasts markedly with the abrupt style of Cato.

There is little to say on the individual personalities. P. Cornelius Scipio Aemilianus Africanus (185/184–129 B.C.), son of L. Aemilius Paulus and adopted son of the elder Scipio, was famous as an orator but otherwise did not actively engage in literature. His friend C. Laelius, called 'the sage', was not only a great orator — some even placed him above Scipio — but also an adept in philosophy; Cicero bears witness to his moderate stoicism. Laelius, though a little older than Scipio, outlived him by several years. His *laudatio funebris* of his dead friend was famous; Scipio's nephew Q. Fabius Maximus made use of it when he had to deliver the public funeral speech. L. Furius Philus (cos. 136 B.C.) had not only philosophical but also antiquarian interests; he was above all an authority on sacred law. Less intimately connected with the circle was Ser. Sulpicius Galba (cos. 144 B.C.), the first orator who consciously employed figures of rhetoric. His fierce temperament made him a most powerful public speaker.

The two poets of the Scipio circle do not fall in this section. Terence was dead when Scipio and Laelius stood in the prime of life, and Lucilius, though a man of their own generation, belongs with his poetry to the following epoch.

It was men of keen and open minds who met in this circle,

Romans who had the courage to accept the full impact of Greek culture, convinced that they would emerge as better Romans. The circle was small and its influence was not widely felt; but it leavened Rome's cultural life for more than a century. Scipio and his friends apparently were not interested in influencing society at large. They might discuss Greek science and philosophy among themselves, but in public they were traditional and conservative. In a critical moment, the general Paulus did employ the astronomical knowledge of his tribune Gallus, but on the whole individual enlightenment did not dispense with the observance of the forms of a magical and primitive religion. Laelius and his two sons-in-law were members of the college of augurs; with Panaetius they would have subscribed to the view, which was later formulated by the Pontifex Q. Mucius Scaevola, that there were three sorts of gods: the gods of the philosophers, of the poets and of the state.

Enlightenment was thus confined within strict limits. Individuals might follow their ideas where they would lead; but the circle as a whole kept within its social class. This is true even of their *humanitas*: the Scipios and their followers, though not blind to the social problems of their time, openly opposed the social reform movement of the Gracchi. As an idea, the Scipionic humanism had far-reaching effects, but the Roman state was on the eve of a hundred-year crisis. In the very same year in which Cicero makes Scipio and his friends meet for a discussion of the state, Scipio died, perhaps the victim of a political murder. His death closed an era: the heyday of the *res publica Romana* had come to an end.

3. From the Gracchi to the Death of Cicero

133–43 B.C.

LITERATURE BETWEEN 133 AND 82 B.C.

ROME had disappointed many who set great hopes on her ascent. The annihilation of Carthage and Corinth showed brutal powers at work; doubts came even to such an enthusiastic admirer of Rome as Polybius. The Pergamenian Kingdom, established in 129 B.C. as the province of Asia, was soon handed over to the greed of the tax-farmers. The social and political reforms of the brothers Ti. and C. Gracchus, achieved not without breaches of the constitution and paid for with the lives of both tribunes, were successfully sabotaged; the continuing grievances of the plebs and the corruption of the senatorial party, especially in the war with Jugurtha (111–105 B.C.), produced and established political demagogues. The *lex iudicaria* of C. Gracchus, who replaced the senators by the knights as jurors in the law courts, encouraged rather than discouraged class justice. Thus P. Rutilius Rufus, who as an official in Asia had made a stand against the tax-farmers, was on his return (92 B.C.) accused of extortion before a jury of knights (men of their own class!), and found guilty; he went into exile and spent the remainder of his days as a guest of the province which he was alleged to have plundered.

Slave rebellions shook the state from within, the invasion of the Cimbri and Teutons from without. In a perilous war the Italians gained Roman civic rights (89 B.C.). In such a time of danger C. Marius, a peasant's son from the region of Arpinum, worked his way to the top; he was consul seven times. The horrible civil war between the people's party of Marius and the *optimates* under L. Cornelius Sulla ended five years after Marius's death with the victory of the Sullans (82 B.C.). Since 133 B.C. political massacre, proscription and control of the courts by political parties were frequent.

The leading politicians were not much interested in literature, Marius positively prided himself on his lack of education. Even Sulla, who had brought the writings of Aristotle and Theo-phrastus from Athens to Rome, who composed Greek epigrams and wrote an extensive autobiography in the hellenistic style, gave but little incentive to intellectual activities except when they were in the service of his policy; under him the history of the earlier period, *e.g.* the class struggle, was rewritten from the senatorial point of view. The theatre, which Sulla liked, became more and more a place of mere entertainment. The poetry of the period seldom achieved greatness; L. Accius and C. Lucilius have their roots in the time of Scipio. Only the art of oratory flourished in the political crisis; historical writing and erudition were also cultivated. These were the formative years of Latin prose, which reached perfection with Caesar and Cicero.

THE ART OF ORATORY

We know the orators of the time from the lively descriptions in Cicero's *Brutus*. He had before him the texts of many speeches now lost; he himself had heard Antonius, Crassus and their con-temporaries. In his work even the scanty quotations come to life.

The self-taught orator gave way to the pupil of the rhetorician, and on the Greek model was formed not only oratory but also the Latin art of prose. The Roman learnt to choose and place his words carefully, to eliminate what was vulgar, archaic or poetic, to organize his ideas and to construct either periods or short colons, which would strike the ear with rhythmic endings (*clausulae*). Besides effective structure and impressive treatment of detail, attention was paid also to delivery and bearing (*actio*).

TI. GRACCHUS (tribune 133 B.C.) had lessons in oratory from a Greek in his home. He possessed natural oratorical talent, but he did not live long enough to develop it as did his one-time supporter C. Papirius Carbo (cos. 120 B.C.), who became famous as a lawyer. A much stronger personality as an orator and a politician was Tiberius's younger brother, C. GRACCHUS (tribune 123 and 122 B.C.). The high praise bestowed on his oratory even by the conservative Cicero is borne out by the fragments of his speeches. Fiery and accomplished, passionate as well as dignified, familiar, through his teacher Menelaos, with the rhetoric of Asia Minor, he could always be sure of his effect. He was a master of that sarcasm which would strike sparks from the exasperation of his audience. His speeches merely lacked polish.

In the history of Latin prose, CORNELIA, the mother of the Gracchi, may also claim a place. From a collection of her letters two fragments remain, both addressed to her son Gaius. There is the pride and loyalty of a Roman matron ; there is also the touching illogicality of a worried mother and widow. This is not literature, but a precious human document.

Among the opponents of C. Gracchus, we find the son-in-law of Laelius, C. Fannius (cos. 122 B.C.). Comrade in arms of Ti. Gracchus before Carthage, he later strongly opposed Gaius's proposals of reform. His speech *De sociis et nomine Latino* (against the proposal to give the Italians Roman citizenship) was famous. Less remarkable as an orator was Scipio's nephew, the lawyer Q. Aelius Tubero. Although a favourite pupil of the moderate Panaetius, he developed into an extremist. His speech, like his manner, was rough and uncompromising (*durus incultus horridus*). Cicero knew a speech of C. Gracchus against him and Tubero's speeches against Gracchus. More remarkable was M. Aemilius Scaurus (cos. 115 B.C.), known as the champion of the *optimates*. Cicero, however, criticizes his lack of elegance and persuasiveness. For P. Rutilius Rufus, as for Tubero, his strict stoicism was a disadvantage on the orator's platform. Both men also wrote their memoirs, undoubtedly in self-defence; perhaps they were the first Romans to do so. There had been precedents in the hellenistic world; Aratus, the general of the Achaean Federation (about 215 B.C.), had published an auto-biography. For Rome such individualism was new, but it quickly set the fashion: the memoirs of Q. Lutatius Catulus (cos. 102 B.C.) and of the dictator Sulla were to follow.

The *eques* C. Titius seems to have stood between these two generations. He is described as a contemporary of Lucilius as well as of Antonius and Crassus. His *argutiae* (precision) and *urbanitas* were praised by Cicero. Titius also wrote tragedies, apparently in a laboured rhetorical style.

In Cicero's youth the forum was dominated by two orators, who, in full possession of the Greek technique and of a Latin prose which had attained maturity, seemed to embody for the young man the ideal of the Roman orator: M. ANTONIUS and L. LICINIUS CRASSUS. They were more or less of the same age (Antonius cos. 99 B.C., Crassus 95 B.C.); Antonius was murdered by the Marians in 87 B.C. Cicero not only recorded his impressions of their skill in his *Brutus*, but also made them the leading speakers in his chief rhetorical work *De Oratore*. In everything that was a matter of training, they were second to no one in their day. Antonius had a lively mind, which reacted swiftly and unfailingly even to the unexpected, and a particu-larly effective delivery; he also knew that the art of the perfect orator lies in concealing his art. Crassus, on the other hand, whom Cicero placed even above Antonius, distinguished him-self by careful diction and *gravitas*; above all he was an incom-parable interpreter of the law. He was known as the defender of the principle of *aequitas* (fairness as opposed to strict observa-tion of the letter of the law); he even won a famous case against the greatest lawyer of his time, the pontifex Q. Mucius Scaevola (cos. 95 B.C., murdered in 82 B.C. by the Marians). None of their contemporaries, not even the cultured L. Marcius Philippus (cos. 91 B.C.), whose ready wit was feared, could measure up to those two. Unfortunately, little of the work of these orators remains. Antonius on purpose did not publish his speeches so that they could not be used as a weapon against him; perhaps he also realized that without his lively delivery they would not have the same effect.

The Roman orators learnt from the Greeks also the theory of oratory, and consciously made more and more use of it. They assimilated the rhetorical teaching of Aristotle and Anaximenes and especially that of Hermagoras of Temnos, who lived in the second century B.C. and whose influence lasted for a long time. There were Greek rhetoricians, *i.e.* professional teachers of eloquence, in Rome even before the middle of the second century; a decree of the senate, of 161 B.C., temporarily expelled them from the city. The penetration of rhetoric was halted as little by this measure as was that of philosophy by similar decrees. The brothers Ti. and C. Gracchus had Greek teachers of eloquence; Antonius carried on rhetorical studies in Athens, Rhodes and Asia Minor. In Cicero's youth to study rhetoric with a Greek teacher was for the Roman a matter of course. The people's party tried to introduce a Latin rhetoric in the place of the Greek one, on Roman models and with a Latin terminology; its first representative was one L. Plotius Gallus. The edict of the censors Cn. Domitius Ahenobarbus and L. Licinius Crassus (92 B.C.) closed this school, ostensibly because it 'was against tradition and established custom', in truth undoubtedly for political reasons. His teaching seems to have continued privately; but it was pointed out to the young Cicero, who would have liked to attend Gallus's courses, that this was not the right place for him. We can form an idea of these *rhetores Latini* from a textbook of rhetoric in four books, dedicated to one C. HERENNIUS; the writer is unknown. The manuscripts ascribe it to Cicero; it is, however, doubtless the work of a man who sympathized with the *populares* (the popular party), and probably dates from between 87 B.C. and 82 B.C. The author bases his work on the system of Hermagoras, but he gives a wide berth to Greek subtleties and confines himself to the essential and practical; he also employs Latin terminology and Latin models and examples. The presentation is clear, but the language is clumsy.

THE PROSE WRITERS

History. — The historians of the time of the Gracchi were interested mostly in writing history of their own time. This is least evident in the work of the earliest among them, L. Calpurnius Piso Frugi, who still belongs to the era of the Scipios (tribune 149 B.C., cos. 133 B.C.). He was fond of rationalizing and of digressions on natural history. Although a conservative nationalist like Cato, he wrote a factual and reliable account of Roman history down to the year 146 B.C. His primitive style, which is characteristic also of Piso's speeches, was not according to Cicero's taste. The *Annales* of Fannius, despite their title, were apparently devoted exclusively to contemporary events. Contemporary history was written also by Sempronius Asellio, who had been military tribune under Scipio at Numantia (134/133 B.C.); his *Historiae*, composed in his old age, extended at least to the year 91 B.C. In the preface, from which a sizeable fragment has been preserved, he describes himself as a pragmatic historian following in the footsteps of Polybius.

There were also historical monographs. L. Coelius Antipater (after 121 B.C.) wrote a history of the second Punic war, which was used by Livy. It was dedicated to L. Aelius Stilo. Antipater used numerous sources, Punic as well as Roman, in order to write objectively; he also shows an interest in countries and peoples, in myths and legends. He wanted to create a prose epic; he therefore strove after attractive presentation and employed rhetorical devices. Cicero bestows on him rather patronizing praise.

The historical writing of Sulla's time shows quite a different picture. Research on sources becomes less important; what matters more is the attractive novelistic presentation. It is now that many of the Roman legends familiar to us get their canonical form. There is also a tendency towards antiquarian detail, which often looks deceptively authentic.

The two most famous annalists of the period, CLAUDIUS QUADRIGARIUS and VALERIUS ANTIAS, were clients of noble families and wrote in the service of their patrons. Claudius, whose work began with the Gallic invasion of 389 B.C., models his style on Coelius Antipater; like the latter he inserts speeches (and also letters) composed by himself. Most unreliable, especially as regards figures, was Valerius Antias, whose *Annales* comprised at least seventy-five books. Livy, who used him, had his suspicions (he checked him always with a second source), yet was not by a long way critical enough.

Not until after Sulla's death, it seems, did an enemy of the *optimates*, C. Licinius Macer (cos. 74 B.C.; committed suicide 66 B.C. when accused of extortion), begin to write. Cicero could find nothing good to say about him either as an orator or as a historian; yet Macer, contrary to the spirit of the time, seems to have studied sources and, to a modest extent, brought a critical judgement to his task.

The years after Sulla's death are also the most probable date of the twelve books of *Historiae* by L. CORNELIUS SISENNA, one of the *optimates* (118–67 B.C.). Despite an inclination towards romance in the manner of some historians of Alexander, he became an important source for the time of Sulla, with whose glorification his work ended, and especially for the Social War. As an experienced officer he was interested in military matters; this emerges even from the surviving fragments, although they are mostly short and are quoted only for their archaic and unusual language. At some earlier date — doubtless in the lifetime of Sulla, who encouraged escapism in literature — Sisenna had translated the *Milesian Fables* of a certain Aristides, short stories n the Decameron style. They remained popular for a long time;

as late as 53 B.C. copies were found on Roman soldiers who had fallen in the battle of Carrhae.

Technical literature. — It is interesting that the senate, after the conquest of Carthage, caused the work of the Carthaginian Mago on plantation management to be officially translated into Latin.

From the extensive juridical literature of the Gracchan period, three books *De Iure Civili* of M. Iunius Brutus deserve mention as the first work of Latin scientific prose in dialogue form. It was a 'catechesis' between father and son.

Closer to literature is philology. Its beginnings in Rome go back to the Pergamenian Crates of Mallos, who in 168 B.C. came to Rome as an envoy and during his stay lectured on grammar. In contrast to the textual criticism of the Alexandrians, Crates was especially concerned with the interpretation of poetry; as a stoic he interpreted it allegorically, and saw in poetry veiled moral or scientific doctrine. Crates made a strong impression, but philological studies in Rome developed slowly. Its first master was L. AELIUS STILO from Lanuvium. He was born in about 150 B.C.; in 100 B.C. he accompanied his distinguished friend, the orator Q. Metellus Numidicus, into exile. His nickname (from *stilus*, slate pencil) he got as a logographer (composer of speeches for others). Stilo too was a stoic; this partly explains his interest in etymology and syntax. He interpreted early literature (*e.g.* the Salian song and the Twelve Tables) with regard to its cultural and historical background; he was also interested in Plautus. His influence was great. Among his pupils were Varro and Cicero.

POETRY

Individualism, criticism and partisanship dominate not only the prose of this period; they are also essential elements of the most important poetry of those years, the *saturae* of C. LUCILIUS. This poetry is quite near to prose; Lucilius, as Horace did later, called his satires *Sermones* ('talk' or 'chats'). The genre which

Lucilius created from earlier beginnings — the most Roman genre of Roman literature — is equally typical of the man and of his time : Lucilius is the first Roman poet of social standing.

The year of Lucilius's birth is unknown. It is certain that he died as an old man in Naples (102/101 B.C.) and that he had seen cavalry service, probably in the *cohors praetoria*, under Scipio at Numantia (134/133 B.C.). He cannot have been much younger than Africanus. They probably grew up in the same neighbourhood ; the Scipios had property at Suessa Aurunca, a small Latin town on the Campanian border, where Lucilius was born. The Lucilii were wealthy ; the poet owned, besides the family estate, an elegant house in Rome, and probably *latifundia* ('ranches' or 'estates') in Sicily. It is not on record that he obtained Roman citizenship, but this may be assumed. His brother Lucius was a senator ; Pompey was related to him on his mother's side. Lucilius the poet seems to have had no ambition to rise to senatorial rank, although his means would have allowed him to do so.

Lucilius was more interested in philosophy than was customary even in the circle of Scipio. He seems to have spent considerable time in Athens ; Clitomachus, head of the Academy from 127/126 B.C. to 110 B.C., dedicated one of his works to him. Politically he sympathized with the Scipios, but this did not prevent him from respecting Ti. Gracchus. He was sensitive to personal attacks ; once he sued an actor who had extemporized against him, but the charge was dismissed. Like so many satirists he was no despiser of women, though a confirmed bachelor. Above all he wanted to be his own master ; this, he tells us, was worth more to him than the whole world.

Lucilius did not turn to satire until after his return from Numantia, when he was a mature man ; he might have felt that he was not suited to the new times. The satires presumably circulated singly among his friends before they were published collectively. Two collections, books 26–30 (after 123 B.C.) and 1–21 (after books 26–30) of the complete edition (made perhaps

1. Ezra in his scriptorium—supposed to be a portrait of
Cassiodorus. From the *Codex Amiatinus*

2. CICERO : a bust in the Vatican Museum

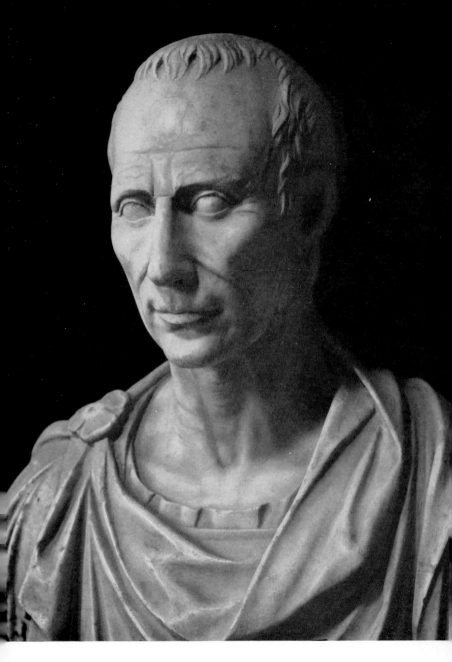

3. CAESAR : a bust in the Vatican Museum

CONTINUOETIISABAUMEUNIQUINCULARETIS.112
DELETHINQAIQUEMODODODEMIASISAQUORAROSTRIS

4. An illustration from the *Vaticanus* of Vergil: Aeneas's ships, in danger of being burned by Turnus and his Rutuli, are transformed into mermaids

eneid, ix. 118-122)

by P. Valerius Cato) had been published by the poet himself; books 22–25 were added posthumously. Some 1300 lines survive; they include a sufficient number of coherent pieces to give some idea of Lucilius's personality and the nature of his satire.

We can even reconstruct the contents of certain books. Book 26 seems to have opened with a dialogue in which Lucilius defends his satiric poetry. To write satire is an urge in him, from which nothing can deflect him; he writes for people who are not too critical, nor yet too simple. The centre-piece of this book was apparently a satire on the plebeian censor of 131 B.C., Q. Caecilius Metellus Macedonicus. In a famous speech (even Augustus invoked it as a precedent for his marriage legislation) Metellus had described marriage as a burden (*molestia*) but at the same time as a patriotic duty; in the same speech he had criticized those who make the gods responsible for their ills. Let us hear what Lucilius made of this: 'Men load their burdens upon themselves: they take wives, beget children so as not to be free from worries. And so I too am out of my mind, I take on myself the duty of procreation.' Metellus was an opponent of Scipio, and the bachelor Lucilius had his own axe to grind. Another theme of the book is parody of tragedies; its victim was probably Accius, whose highflown style and small stature were as welcome targets for Lucilius as were his attempts to reform the spelling of Latin. In book 28 a banquet of Athenian philosophers is described, but also a Roman lover's exploits, much in the style of the *palliata* (*e.g.* a house is taken by storm). Book 30 has a little of everything: there is the fable of the fox and the lion, the portrait of a man who is wax in the hands of his vain and unfaithful wife, polemics against a writer of comedy, description of a banquet, and perhaps a dig at the destruction of the allied town Fregellae, 125 B.C.; if so, this was certainly in the spirit of Scipio, who in his lifetime had stood up for the Italians. He is probably also the great general and friend of the allies on whom the poet lavishes his praise.

Book 1 describes with epic parody (of Naevius and Ennius)

a convention of the gods. Out of care for Rome, they decree the death of L. Cornelius Lentulus Lupus, who, although condemned in 154 B.C. for extortion, nevertheless became *princeps senatus* ('leader of the senate') in 131 B.C.; among the speakers is the immortalized Romulus, who complains of the moral decadence of his people. Book 2 is a court trial: T. Albucius had in 119/118 B.C. accused Q. Mucius Scaevola of extortion and other indictable actions during his praetorship in Asia (121/120 B.C.), but Scaevola was acquitted. Lucilius seems to have contrasted the two opponents also as a stoic and an epicurean. Book 3, the 'Sicilian journey', inspired Horace to write his *Iter Brundisinum* (*Sat.* I, 5). The parallel, but also the individual treatment of either poet, can be followed up even in detail. Lucilius travels with a retinue, to Capua by land, then by sea. His account is given in the form of a letter to a friend who is planning a similar journey. Lucilius seems to have described also some episodes of his journey, *e.g.* a gladiatorial fight and his stay at the house of a Syrian landlady. Quotations from later books are less numerous, but sufficient to prove that their contents were no less diversified: reproach to a friend who neglected to visit the poet when ill, description of a miser who does not let his money-bag out of his hand day or night, the cosmetics of a courtesan of the name of Phryne, literary criticism, scorn of superstition, the tasteless banquet of the town-crier Granius, and moral exhortations. Politics and war get their fair share; L. Opimius, corrupted by Jugurtha, was named in book 11, and book 14 tells of a general in Spain and his quaestor P. Pavus, who mutually complain about one another.

Lucilius's language is extremely powerful and lively; every word hits home. But he is not choosy about his expressions. He does not want to be a purist; he writes everyday language (*sermo cotidianus*), sometimes even soldiers' slang (*sermo castrensis*); with a freedom and carelessness reminiscent of Plautus he mixes Greek and Latin. Coarse, and occasionally obscene, language was traditional in satire, and Lucilius would have forfeited much of his effect had he renounced it.   But the criticism of Horace who took exception to Lucilius's habit of leaving an idea in its raw state as it hit his mind, to the improvised form lacking aesthetic self-criticism, is not unjustified.   Yet Horace bowed to the genius of the satirist; in his *Sermones* he often took issue with Lucilius, and even imitated Lucilian themes in his own, more urbane, style of satire.   There were readers who put Lucilius before Horace, and who actually described him as the greatest Roman poet;   at any rate, the later Roman satire, not only of Seneca and Petronius, but also of Juvenal, is nearer to Lucilius than to Horace.

In the oldest books (26–29) Lucilius still used, like Ennius before him, varied metres (iambic six-foot, trochaic seven-foot) ; from book 30 onwards he uses the hexameter exclusively, which now became the rule for poetical satire.   The elegiac couplet on a slave in book 22 was found among his papers ; it was hardly intended for the collection of satires.

Horace saw in Lucilius the inventor of satire.   Certainly Horace knew the *Saturae* of Ennius, and also those of Pacuvius ; he presumably knew that there were pieces by Naevius and Pomponius with the title *Satura*.   But Lucilius was the first to write satire as it has since been written.   He took over the variety of metres and themes ; he soon gave up the former, but retained the latter.   The variety of contents, the easy transition from one subject to another, is characteristic of satire, especially of Roman satire ; this gives it the appearance of conversation. With regard to themes, Lucilius so limited his satire that its variety of contents blended harmoniously.   All the facets of his satirical art — good-natured humour and bitter sarcasm, irony and invective, smiling wisdom and the preaching of the street philosopher — ultimately aim at the reader's education.   This serio-comic art, which often uses dialogue form, is not incapable of a higher tone, as in Lucilius's exhortation to *virtus*.

Despite the Greek stimulus, Roman satire is linked to native tradition.   It is as different from the comedy of Eupolis, Cratinus and Aristophanes (whom Horace names as Lucilius's models) as it is from the iambics of Archilochus or of Callimachus, even if personal attack is common to all. Like its name, its spirit and style are Roman.

The theatre began to decline. The great dramatists of the second century B.C. were already thought of as 'classics'; their works were again produced, perhaps better than in their lifetime, but there were no more writers of their stature. The last master of the *palliata*, Turpilius, who like Terence imitated Greek models with freedom in details, died in 103 B.C. at a ripe old age. Only Accius, whose *Tereus* was produced in about 104 B.C., was still active in Sulla's time. Beside the *togata*, which fashioned itself more and more after the *palliata*, there was now a literary form of the Oscan farce, the *atellana*. This was characteristic of the generation of the Social War. Even the *atellana* had conformed in some measure to the accepted types of comedy, *palliata* and *togata*. Sulla liked the *atellana* and sponsored it as a form of escapism. Soon the *atellana* had a rival in the literary mime, which dominated the stage in the time of Caesar.

Still under Sulla, CN. MATIUS wrote *mimiambi* in 'limping' iambics, realistic sketches after the manner of Herondas. Gellius quotes about a dozen lines; the language is original (popular but not vulgar), and the few samples surprise by their wealth of themes and nuances of expression.

Matius also translated the *Iliad* into Latin; as far as we can see, he did so in close adherence to the original and not without a sense of the Homeric style. An original epic was the little-known *Bellum Histricum* of Hostius (probably the Istrian campaign of C. Sempronius Tuditanus, 129 B.C.); it seems to have continued the Roman-Homeric tradition created by Ennius.

Something new is the cultivation of the miniature forms of hellenistic literature. Two epigrams by Q. Lutatius Catulus (cos. 102 B.C.) survive. The theme of the first, imitating

Callimachus, is the reluctant yielding of the lover; in the second the rising star of the young actor Roscius is compared with the ascending Aurora. We also know erotic epigrams by Valerius Aedituus, Pompilius, and Porcius Licinus; these light-hearted poems were then already fashionable. More pretentious were the *Erotopaegnia* of Laevius in various lyrical metres; he took his themes from mythology. Such attempts foreshadow the school of the Neoterici.

CICERO AND HIS TIME (82–43 B.C.)

The years between Sulla's dictatorship and the second Triumvirate (82–43 B.C.) can truly be called the age of Cicero. In Cicero the culture of an epoch reached perfection. His person linked the Scipio era, whose youngest representatives he knew, with the Augustan, whose leading personalities grew up in his later years; at a turning-point of history he ensured historical continuity; among his contemporaries he was a mediator between political extremes. And although he died finally as the victim of a lost cause, he coined in thought and word the formulas of a new order, and created the climate in which it could thrive.

Sulla's hope, to have given the Romans 'peace in our time', was not to be fulfilled. Shortly after his death (78 B.C.) disturbances began anew; after twelve years nothing remained of his legislation. The mismanagement in the provinces went on even after the massacre of the Italians in Asia (88 B.C.). Sertorius's attempt to found an independent state in Spain on Roman lines, which might have pointed the way from the colonial empire to a commonwealth, was crushed (80–72 B.C.). External and internal dangers compelled the senate to give one military command after another to Pompey, who was as ambitious as he was gifted in strategy; the intransigence of the senate, who had just emerged from the Catiline crisis, drove the general, returning from the East after unprecedented successes, into the arms of

Caesar, the leader of the popular party. Their alliance could not possibly last. Victory in the civil war gave Caesar a free hand; in his great plans he underestimated only one thing: the republican opposition, to which he fell a victim. It needed another civil war to make a resigned world prefer peace and personal security to freedom. This was the background of Cicero's mature years.

M. TULLIUS CICERO

Cicero is the only Roman of the classical period of whom an authentic biography can be written. As sources we have the extensive self-testimonies in his work, biographies by contemporaries, but above all Cicero's surviving correspondence (over eight hundred pieces) from 68 B.C. until shortly before his death. This was first published in separate collections from Cicero's archives and those of his friends (letters to Pompey, Caesar, Octavian, to his brother Quintus, to his son Marcus, to Cornelius Nepos, etc.). They were apparently edited by Cicero's private secretary, the freedman M. Tullius Tiro. Of this edition, the sixteen books *ad familiares* (among them ninety letters to Cicero from others) and the three books *ad Quintum* remain. Even more informative are the letters to Atticus, in sixteen books; they were not published until at least a hundred years after Cicero's death.

In these letters the whole man stands before us. We experience with him every slight fluctuation in day-to-day politics, the whole gamut of fear and hope in the ups and downs of his career, his pride in success, his despondency in misfortune; we also recognize his seriousness and nobility of mind and his sincere concern for the state and people. We see the author at work as he conceives plans and rejects them, executes and alters them. We find a man who is devotedly attached to his family and friends, who also cares for the slaves of his household. We learn to understand the almost superhuman efforts which it cost a *novus homo* to achieve and maintain his place in leading circles;

and the burden of status, forcing a man of moderate fortune to live beyond his means. But above all we meet an unusually active mind, which draws from literature and art, philosophy and science the strength for an active life which by convention and philosophical conviction he felt to be his duty.

Cicero came from a little-known country family of equestrian rank. He was born in Arpinum, the home of Marius, on 3rd January, 106 B.C. The boy grew up in moderate prosperity, in a home atmosphere of kindly discipline, conservative outlook and a puritan style of living. His father valued Greek culture; a stoic named Diodotus was a friend of the family. Young Marcus found it easy — almost too easy, one might think — to make this tradition his own.

Cicero received his higher education in Rome, under the eyes of the last survivors of the Scipionic era; he studied under L. Aelius Stilo, had conversations with the tragedian Accius, and especially cultivated the company of the two Scaevolae, first of the augur and, after his death, of the pontifex, who were both famous jurists. Through the augur Scaevola, Cicero got to know T. Pomponius Atticus; with him he struck up a lifelong friendship. Soon Scaevola's son-in-law, the great orator L. Crassus, began to take an interest in Cicero. The common attractions of a great city were lost on the purposeful young man; his strongest urges were a zeal for learning, and the ambition to play a role in public life. He later said of himself, not without pride, that he was elected to all offices at the minimum legal age. On Cicero's oratorical education the strongest influence was exercised by a certain Molo of Rhodes, who was then staying at Rome.

Even in a work of his early years, Cicero demands of the orator *sapientia*, that is, general, and especially philosophical, formation. Accordingly, we see Cicero from an early time occupied with philosophical studies. He attended lectures of the epicurean Phaedrus, who made little impression on him, of the academic Philo of Larisa, and later in Greece and Asia Minor of the famous stoic Posidonius and the eclectic Antiochus of Ascalon. Nor did he neglect literature; beside tragedy and comedy he liked Lucilius, but above all 'our' ('*noster*') Ennius.

Still under Sulla (80 B.C.), Cicero defended the young Sextus Roscius from Ameria, who was accused of patricide. The political background of the false accusation was an open secret; but with Chrysogonus, the powerful favourite of Sulla, behind the scene, none of the well-known lawyers dared to intervene for Roscius. Cicero, not yet politically committed, undertook the defence. He wisely dissociated Sulla, the saviour of the state, from his minions, in whose society the real murderer was to be found, and movingly conjured up before the eyes of the jury the sad fate of Roscius, exiled, driven from home, now threatened with a cruel death penalty. Despite its youthful exuberance the oration had great success, and achieved the client's acquittal. It is interesting that Cicero even at this stage, for all his praise of Sulla's restoration, finds impressive words for the sinister weapon of proscription.

Cicero did not yet feel master of his art. He had a tendency towards exuberance in expression and delivery. To perfect his style and technique he went to Greece and Asia Minor in 79–77 B.C. Perhaps he also felt that Rome had grown too hot for the defender of Roscius. He once more studied seriously under Molo; he also kept up his keen interest in philosophy. In Smyrna he made the acquaintance of the famous Rutilius Rufus.

From 76 B.C. Cicero was again busy as a lawyer in Rome. During his Sicilian quaestorship (75 B.C.) he won the confidence of the Sicilians. He also found time for his cultural pursuits. In his old age he still recalled, not without a dash of pride, how he rediscovered the grave of Archimedes, forgotten by the Syracusans and overgrown by brambles. Reactionary *optimates* like L. Metellus took offence at his speaking Greek in the town hall of Syracuse. On his departure he offered the Sicilians his good services in any emergency; he was soon to have an opportunity to keep his word. In the year 70 B.C. C. Verres, who as pro-praetor 73-71 B.C. had shamelessly plundered and harassed the Sicilians, had to answer a charge of extortion. Cicero, then candidate for the aedileship, secured his appointment as prosecuting counsel against Q. Caecilius, who had been put up by friends of Verres. The incriminating evidence which Cicero produced was so weighty that Verres's counsel, the famous Q. Hortensius, renounced his client's defence. Verres, seeing his case lost, went into voluntary exile before the verdict was returned. Cicero had become the foremost orator in Rome. In order to consolidate this reputation he published five further speeches against Verres from the vast material not used in the trial.

To make his way into the leading political circles was not easy for Cicero. The *nobiles* looked down on the *novus homo*; they would hardly be impressed by his education, but were quite prepared to make use of the idealism and power of words of a man who neither could nor would play their game. It needed the ambition and the single-mindedness of Cicero to go ahead unperturbed. In the year 67 B.C. he was elected praetor; at that time he had just acquired the first of his country estates, his beloved Tusculanum. As praetor (66 B.C.) Cicero spoke for the proposal of the tribune C. Manilius to extend the command of Pompey to the whole of Asia. Cicero needed the friendship of the powerful man; the people of the class from which he came, the knights, saw their interests in Asia threatened by the half-hearted warfare of the *optimates* against Mithridates. Also under Cicero's praetorship falls the beginning of Catiline's conspiracy. Three years later, when the Catilinarians were ready to launch their attack, Cicero was consul. He stood at his desired goal. His discovery and crushing of the conspiracy was the climax but also the tragic turning-point of his life.

The electoral year 64 B.C. was marked for Cicero by the death of his father, the birth of his son Marcus and the first marriage of his daughter Tullia (with C. Piso). His brother Quintus, who despite some differences of opinion was always close to him, wrote for him his treatise on the candidacy for consulship, a revealing political document of the times. Cicero borrowed some of his brother's ideas in the speech he made as a candidate.

Best known among the speeches of his consular year are the four against Catiline. The first and the third were not delivered exactly as Cicero later published them. The famous first speech (*Quousque tandem* . . .) was originally an improvisation. In that moment of danger Cicero had the support of all those who wished public order to be maintained; but the political tension made it impossible to put his programme of integration (*concordia ordinum*, the harmonious working together of the classes) into effect.

Three years later the saviour of Rome found himself isolated. The *optimates*, annoyed by his leaning towards Pompey, cut him dead; his old opponents, the *populares*, had a weapon against him in the constitutionally debatable death-sentence passed on the leading Catilinarians. Cicero made spasmodic attempts to break through his isolation, but without success.

At first Cicero looked out for literary propagandists. His speech for the contested citizenship of the Greek poet Archias (62 B.C.), rightly famous as a testimony of the *humanitas Ciceroniana*, was calculated to win this favourite of high society for his cause. In the years 60–59 B.C. he published his (revised) consular orations. As late as the year 56 B.C., Cicero was trying to get the historian L. Lucceius to compose a panegyrical history of his consulate in the hellenistic manner. It remained a promise. Cicero had to fend for himself. He composed a Greek account of his consulate, followed by an 'inside story'; and as no poet would praise him, he wrote his own encomium: *De suo consulatu*, followed (about 55 B.C.) by *De temporibus suis*, in three books. His lack of taste in writing a poetical self-glorification got on the nerves even of Cicero's contemporaries, who were used to self-praise.

Apart from these two epics Cicero composed, among other poems, a (lost) epic *Marius* and a verse translation of the *Phaenomena* ('heavenly signs') of the stoic astronomer Aratus (died

240 B.C.). If Cicero was no genuine poet, his own verse and his translations from Greek poetry give him a place in the development of the Latin verse technique and poetic language.

Pompey, abruptly dismissed by the senate, had joined the leaders of the *populares*, Caesar and Crassus, in the 'Triumvirate' of the year 60 B.C. Caesar tried to enlist Cicero, but the latter kept aloof. He soon had to suffer for it. Under a retroactive law of the tribune P. Clodius, Cicero was punished for the unconstitutional execution of Roman citizens with exile and the loss of civic rights; his house on the Palatine and his villas (he already had several) were destroyed, and his property confiscated. Cicero did not bear his misfortune with much dignity. The letters written in exile (at Dyrrhachium on the Dalmatian coast) are full of self-pity, of complaints about false friends (real or imagined), and of attempts to get influential persons in Rome to plead his case. In mid-57 B.C. Cicero at last succeeded: on the proposal of the tribunes P. Sestius and T. Annius Milo he was unanimously recalled. His homecoming was like a triumph.

Cicero had learned one thing: the old order was not capable of renovation. In the orations of these years (*e.g. pro Sestio*, 56 B.C.) Cicero no longer demanded the co-operation of the classes (*concordia ordinum*), but the *consensus omnium bonorum*, the concentration of all constructive forces in the state: along with those *nobiles* who deserved their name, all capable and well-disposed men, especially those of the equestrian order, from whom the *novus homo* had come, were to be called upon. They were the true *optimates*, pioneers and leaders (*principes*) like Plato's statesman; in a crisis the *rector et gubernator rei publicae* (ruler and helmsman of the state) should come forward, endowed with exceptional energy and judgement (this too a Platonic ideal) to rescue the state as a *dictator*.

Cicero now approached Caesar, and hoped to win him for the 'good cause'. Disgusted by the political unrest, he withdrew into private life. In theoretical works (*De oratore, De re publica, De legibus*) he explained the ideas of his latest speeches and developed them.

De oratore (55 B.C.), a dialogue in three books, with Antonius and Crassus as principal speakers, portrays the political orator who is not only master of his art but is also philosophically educated. In book 1 Crassus speaks of the prerequisites of the oratorical vocation: talent, training, technique, knowledge of the law; above all common sense. In book 2 Antonius gives an exposé of rhetoric in the narrower sense, setting forth and explaining its essential points. Book 3 treats of style (*elocutio*) and delivery (*actio*) but also contains a long digression by Crassus, who insists on the philosophical training of the orator.

The subject of the 'Republic' and 'Laws' is political philosophy. Both follow Plato in their theme, but in their details are indebted to later philosophy, especially Dicaearchus, who placed the active life above the speculative life; Cicero speaks about Roman politics from his own experience. *De re publica* poses the question of the best form of government and the best citizen; the conversation, in which leading men of the Scipio circle take part, is placed in the year 129 B.C. The state (*res publica*) is the affair of the people (*res populi*). It originates in an inborn striving for harmonious fellowship (*concordia*, the stoic *homonoia*). In the first book the well-known basic forms of government and their caricatures are set forth. Book 2 gives a short history of the Roman constitution. With book 3 the systematic exposition begins. The fundamental element of government is justice, a concept which Cicero critically examines and defends. In book 4 he designs a model state, but not so rigorous as Plato's; *e.g.* he defends poetry and drama as a mirror of life. Cicero's ideal state is an idealized Roman state. In the discussion of the *optimus civis*, too (books 4–6), Cicero takes up his own political thoughts. For Cicero the ideal politician is just the best among the good; he is sole ruler only in the gravest crisis, and even then he rules constitutionally. Cicero deliberately calls him here *rector*, not *princeps*; the 'first citizen' must always restore the traditional constitution. Cicero's helmsman of the state wants no worldly reward, and no fame; his reward is immortality. This idea leads to Scipio's dream, in which the dreamer sees his ancestor, the victor over Hannibal, and — a typically Roman counterpart to the vision of the world beyond the grave of the Armenian Er in Plato — gets a glimpse of a world in which the great and the good live eternally in blissful contemplation of the harmony of the universe.

De legibus (the remaining three books were written some time after 52 B.C.; the continuation, of unknown extent, is lost) sets out to be a counterpart to Plato's 'Laws'. Yet even more so than in the *De re publica* Cicero is in thought and matter independent of Plato. The surviving books deal with natural law, sacred law and the laws of the magistrates; the continuation dealt with law courts and apparently also (as did Plato) with education. The dialogue is placed in Cicero's own time; the people taking part in the conversation are himself, Quintus and Atticus.

Siding with the Triumvirs meant for Cicero many a personal humiliation; he defended, for example, his old opponent Vatinius (54 B.C.). Tullia had contracted a third marriage with the Caesarian P. Cornelius Dolabella, of whom her father thought little as a person. But in the same year, 54 B.C., Cicero accepted from Caesar a loan of 800,000 sesterces which he desperately needed. On the other hand, he had the satisfaction of being chosen for the Augural College in place of Crassus, who had fallen in the war with the Parthians in 53 B.C. The following year, however, brought a new disappointment with the unsuccessful defence of his friend Milo.

Milo had been trying for years to hold in check the terrorizing band of Clodius with an opposing band. At the beginning of 52 B.C. the two had a fight on the Via Appia; Clodius was wounded and fled to a tavern, but Milo had him dragged out and killed by his followers. At the burial of Clodius there were turbulent demonstrations. Pompey, appointed consul without a colleague, had Milo brought to trial. His soldiers occupied the forum; Cicero spoke without self-confidence and his words were drowned by the noise of the excited crowd. Having no doubts about his conviction, Milo went voluntarily into exile. Cicero, disappointed with his failure, worked out a new defence speech and sent it to Milo in Massilia. Milo answered ironically that if Cicero had defended him so successfully he would not now be able to eat such good Massilian food. The speech counted in antiquity as Cicero's oratorical masterpiece. His skill in pleading a hopeless case is really astonishing; but even under more favourable circumstances his attempt to represent Milo's deed as self-defence would have had little prospect of success.

In 51 B.C. the ex-consul went on his long overdue provincial year. As proconsul of Cilicia he showed himself just and humane. He also had some military success against the Parthians. His pathetic endeavours to be granted a triumph for it are perhaps not to be put down merely to his well-known vanity; he urgently needed public recognition. He was at least permitted to celebrate a feast of thanksgiving (*supplicatio*); the decision on the triumph for which he hoped was never reached: the Roman world was on the verge of a new civil war.

Nothing could have been more horrible to Cicero. To the end he tried to mediate between the opponents. He no longer had illusions about Pompey, but in Caesar, with all his esteem for his person, he saw the future destroyer of the republic. So he fled from Caesar (June 49 B.C.) to the camp of Pompey. What he saw there did not please him; he felt out of place and made himself unpopular as a fault-finder. After the annihilating defeat of Pompey at Pharsalos (48 B.C.) he returned to Italy, where Caesar treated him graciously.

Most of the time to the end of the civil war was spent by Cicero in retirement; it was again a period of intensive writing. In 46 B.C. he produced the rhetorical writings *Brutus, Orator, Paradoxa Stoicorum* and an encomium of the stoic Cato; all are dedicated to M. Iunius Brutus, who, originally an opponent of

Caesar, had gone over to his side in 48 B.C. and now enjoyed his confidence.

Brutus is a conversation between Brutus, Atticus and the main speaker, Cicero. The latter, starting with the death of Hortensius (50 B.C.), sketches the history of Roman eloquence from its beginnings to his own time ; as in later works, he lets his own merits be complimented by the other speakers. Bitterness about the new regime is in evidence from the start: Hortensius was lucky not to have lived to see the death of free speech, which is the prerequisite of all oratory. Similar political animosity is found in the *Paradoxa Stoicorum*, which Cicero counted among his rhetorical writings. In this work he treats some of the commonplaces of popular philosophy from the point of view of the orator.

In *Brutus* Cicero had already had occasion to criticize the one-sided 'Atticist' style, to which Brutus subscribed. This literary fashion at Rome in the mid-century was a reaction against the florid Asiatic style, under whose influence the early Roman oratory and even Hortensius and the young Cicero had been. But the 'Atticists' went too far for Cicero's taste; their one and only ideal was the 'simple' Lysias. Cicero preferred a mixture of the plain, the moderate and the rich style ; he saw this ideal fulfilled in Demosthenes. This is the theme of the *Orator*, a work without political undertones. All the more Cicero insists on his old demand: that the orator must not neglect philosophy. He expressed himself similarly in a minor work, *De optimo genere oratorum*.

The speeches of the years 46 and 45 B.C. are appeals to Caesar's mercy on behalf of one-time Pompeians or thanks for their reprieve. The appeal to Caesar's kindness and generosity had surprising success in the case of Q. Ligarius (46 B.C.), but failed in the defence of the Galatian prince Deiotarus ; Cicero's persistent exhortation to restore the republic annoyed the dictator.

A great deal was happening also in Cicero's private life. For some time past his relations with his ambitious wife, Terentia, had been rather cool; he separated from her in 46 B.C. and soon married the much younger Publilia, a rich heiress, probably in the hope that he could then pay off his debt to Caesar. In February 45 B.C. Tullia, just separated from Dolabella, died, shortly after the birth of a son. The death of his beloved daughter hit Cicero hard; for the first time, so he himself admits, he felt crushed by fate. Restlessly he went from one of his estates to the other; in between he stayed with Atticus. He neglected his young wife and soon divorced her. As time went on, he found consolation in philosophy. His *Consolatio*, in contrast to its more or less conventional models, is the first book of its kind written for the author's own consolation. It was followed by *Hortensius*, an encouragement of the study of philosophy. Both works are lost.

Hortensius was only a prelude. The idea was now ripening in Cicero to introduce Greek philosophy to Latin-speaking readers in a series of larger works. In the years 45/44 B.C. fall the *Academica, De finibus bonorum et malorum, Tusculanae disputationes*, and the *De natura deorum*, probably also the translations of Plato's *Protagoras* and *Timaeus*. Their effect on Cicero's contemporaries was slight; whoever had philosophical interests at that time read the Greeks in the original. The Roman Christians later drew from these writings their knowledge of ancient philosophy, and the Renaissance finally made them a common property of European culture.

Having once entered the circle of Caesar, Cicero had no possibility of evading the ever more frequent and subservient acts of homage to the uncrowned king. It was only natural that in his thoughts he should hark back to the 'great time': in this mood he wrote his *Cato maior de senectute*, which after Caesar's murder was followed by *Laelius de amicitia*. Both are dedicated to his friend Atticus.

The former is a conversation between the old Cato, Laelius and the younger Scipio. The appeal of this work comes not from its theme, which only reproduces philosophical common-places, but from the loving portrayal, idealized, but not beyond recognition, of Cato. *Laelius* is more problematical. The theme — nature, obligations and limits of friendship — is developed on a stoic-peripatetic basis by Laelius in conversation with his sons-in-law, C. Fannius and the augur Scaevola, shortly after the death of the younger Scipio (129 B.C.); Cicero has allegedly heard a report from Scaevola; in actual fact, he is here project-ing into an analogous situation of the past his own feeling that the world around him has changed. A large place is given to the question of how far personal friendship is compatible with political opposition, a question which just then weighed heavily on his mind.

The unexpected news of Caesar's assassination came to Cicero as a relief. The pent-up dislike of the man whose charm he had been unable to resist now burst forth unrestrained. But the course of events soon crushed his hopes. Brutus and his fol-lowers had missed the moment for action. Cicero wanted at first to go to Athens where he had sent his son Marcus to study, but allowed himself to be persuaded by friends to stay. His last hope was now, through the support of Caesar's heir Octavian and the Caesarians who stood by him, to isolate the unscrupulous Antony and have him declared an enemy of the state. Evidence of this policy is a group of speeches which Cicero himself play-fully called *Philippics*. The fourteen which survive fall between 2nd September 44 B.C., and 22nd April 43 B.C.: they are all, directly or indirectly, aimed at Antony. Once again, especially in the third and fourth *Philippics* (both 20th December 44 B.C.), Cicero outlines, with all the power of his eloquence, his old programme. Even in the philosophical works which he wrote between Caesar's assassination and his own re-entry into politics he is again concerned with problems of action. In *De divinatione* he insists on the difference between religion and superstition; in *De fato* he defends free will against destiny; *De offiiics*, dedi-cated to his son Marcus, is a system of applied ethics and at the

D

same time a justification of his own actions. For his Laelius, too, friendship that was to last had to be based on *virtus*.

The large philosophical works of the years 45–43 B.C. might well have been planned as a series. His *Academici libri* were revised several times. The first version consisted of two books, which were named after the principal characters, Catulus and Lucullus; only the second book survives. Of a later version, in which Cicero brings in his friend Varro, we still have the beginning of the first book and a few fragments. *De finibus* (about the highest good and the greatest evil) and the *Tusculanae* (both works of five books, dedicated to Brutus) discuss questions of ethics. *De finibus* shows the attitudes of the philosophical schools to this fundamental problem. Cicero's natural sympathies are with the stoics, although rationally he inclines towards the scepticism of the academics; only to Epicurus is he less than fair. The *Tusculanae* are devoted to specific questions of philosophy: death is not an evil (1), pain is bearable (2), disturbances of one's peace of mind (*aegritudo* and *perturbatio animi*) can be alleviated (3–4), virtue is sufficient for a happy life (5). Here too, Cicero sympathizes with the stoics, without entirely accepting their point of view. In both works Cicero is the principal speaker. *De natura deorum* (three books, the last incomplete) has the form of a conversation which Cicero says he had in 77 B.C. with the epicurean C. Velleius, the stoic Q. Lucilius Balbus and the academic (also a famous orator) C. Aurelius Cotta. Velleius sets forth the epicurean view, Balbus the stoic; after each Cotta speaks, and refutes both. In *De divinatione*, Cicero, as augur, discusses with his brother the nature of augury; in the first book the stoic teaching, which endeavours to justify augury on philosophical grounds, is set forth after Posidonius, and in the second book it is refuted. The reader is also allowed some glimpses of the art of augury as seen, not without humour, by an enlightened and sceptical augur. The first two books of *De officiis* are an abbreviated rendering of a work of Panaetius 'On correct behaviour'; book 1 treats of the honourable (*honestum*), book 2 of the expedient (*utile*) as motives of the ethical decision, book 3 of the conflict of the two. (More than other works of Cicero's this one found readers among the Christians; Ambrose was inspired by it to write his work *De officiis ministrorum*.) Half rhetorical, half philosophical are the *Topica*, written in 44 B.C. on a sea voyage from Velia to Rhegium.

Cicero still believed himself to be in the centre of events. Octavian, however, had already come to a secret understanding with Antony and Lepidus. Antony insisted on the proscription of his hated opponent, and Octavian, hesitantly and against his will, gave in. On 7th December 43 B.C. Cicero was assassinated; he met his fate with composure. His head and hands were cut off and taken to Antony; he put them on show in Rome. In his later years, however, Octavian admitted to his grandson that Cicero was not only a great orator but also a patriot.

Cicero's speeches — fifty-seven survive, some thirty more are known to have existed — impress not only by their oratorical qualities, but above all by their spiritual and human substance. In this respect Cicero rises as far above his contemporaries, as his mature style eclipses that of the Asians and Atticists. The bitterness (and lack of taste) of his invective was common in Rome at the time; his self-praise — excessive, if not entirely unfounded — is understandable from his character and his life.

Cicero's oratorical style changed more than once. His earliest speeches are strongly Asiatic, the speech *pro Roscio comoedo* is quite in the style of Hortensius; Cicero is not yet the purist which the speeches of the best period (from his praetorship to the civil war) show him to be. Later, in the *Orationes Caesarianae* and *Philippicae*, he makes again some concessions to a less rigorous style.

Cicero's speeches are permeated with philosophical thought. Even though it is presented in a conventional form, it amounts to more than a string of commonplaces. Of course, Cicero is not a philosopher in the strictest meaning of the term, but he does show a serious interest in philosophy, especially when applied to practical questions. Characteristically his philosophizing begins with the state, and with the orator as a statesman. For this reason alone Cicero could never have been an epicurean; Epicurus's maxim 'live in private' would have seemed to him a betrayal of his *humanitas*. Yet the dogmatism of the stoics suited him as little as did the hedonism of Epicurus.

As a philosophical writer Cicero was neither a mere translator, nor a popularizer. He himself appropriately compared his *Philosophica* with the Roman adaptations of Greek drama. If he has not penetrated the last subtleties of philosophical controversy, if he does not always keep to the best and most authentic sources, if his presentation is not free from misunderstanding and carelessness (two such extensive works as the *Tusculanae* and the *De finibus* were written in little more than a year), he gave his difficult subject a perfect form: he made Latin a medium for abstract thought, and created in the numerous historical examples, episodes, and anecdotes a narrative style of great excellence.

Cicero's work as a whole is imbued with the spirit of that *humanitas* which we first meet in the circle of Scipio and for which Cicero himself is our most outstanding witness and interpreter. In fact, we cannot help seeing it through Cicero's eyes. It is through his work that it affected, directly or indirectly, the middle ages and the Renaissance. Seen as a whole, this is perhaps the strongest effect which Cicero had; it can be compared only with that of Vergil.

PROSE IN CICERO'S ENVIRONMENT

What the average prose of the time was like may be learnt from Cicero's correspondents. There are the Atticists M. Brutus and Asinius Pollio, but also stylists of Cicero's sort like M. Caelius Rufus, who was also his pupil as an orator, or L. Munatius Plancus. Of the numerous orators among Cicero's contemporaries unfortunately almost nothing survives. For the most famous of them, the 'Asiatic' Q. HORTENSIUS HORTALUS, we depend almost entirely on Cicero's judgement. From the time when the nineteen-year-old spoke before the consuls Crassus and Scaevola in 95 B.C., he was the most successful and admired orator until Cicero put him somewhat in the shade. Now as opponents in court, now as colleagues (*e.g.* as defenders of Milo), the two were always friends. Cicero admired in Hortensius above all his astonishing memory. From the time of his consulate (69 B.C.) Hortensius tended to be rather easy-going; it needed the consular speeches of Cicero to stimulate him to new exertions. But the Asiatic style to which he stuck was not so suitable in his later years as it had been in his youth. His daughter Hortensia made a stir when in 42 B.C. she spoke with success before the Triumviri against the taxation of women's property. A less skilful orator was C. Licinius Calvus, also a poet. M. Cato (95–46 B.C.), in spite of being a stoic, was a speaker of some merit.

M. TERENTIUS VARRO

VARRO of Reate (116–27 B.C.) is the most versatile author of his time next to Cicero, with whom he had many if not very close connexions. Insignificant as an orator (Asiatic), original as a philosophical author and writer of *saturae*, he was above all a scholar of universal interests. He inclined slightly to the Pythagorean mysticism which was becoming fashionable at the time. An officer of Pompey in the civil war, he had to surrender in Spain in 49 B.C. Caesar appointed him head of a public library which he was planning. He escaped Antony's proscription (43 B.C.) through the intervention of a friend.

Varro's writings, over six hundred books, were much studied, and used by compilers, to the end of antiquity; they themselves have almost all perished, but the fruits of Varro's research are largely surviving.

Only a few of his works can be mentioned here. There is

the *Antiquitates* in forty-one books (twenty-five *libri rerum humanarum*, sixteen *rerum divinarum*), an encyclopaedia of Roman antiquities. The *res divinae*, dedicated to Caesar as Pontifex Maximus and probably published in the year 47 B.C., are an important source for Roman religion. In connexion with the *Antiquitates* Varro wrote some smaller works, *e.g. De vita populi Romani* (cultural history) and *De gente populi Romani*, an attempt to place Rome in the mythological tradition of the Greeks. A system of chronology which dates the foundation of Rome at 753 B.C. probably goes back to Varro; it was taken over by Atticus and came to be universally accepted. The *Hebdomades* or *Imagines* (completed about 39 B.C.) were a collection of seven hundred portraits of famous personalities (Greek and Roman kings, generals, politicians, poets, etc.) with accompanying text in prose and verse. There were a hundred groups of seven 'pictures' each. — The *Disciplinarum libri IX* are in the tradition of that encyclopaedic learning which had developed from earlier beginnings in hellenism. Varro treated of grammar, dialectics, rhetoric, geometry, arithmetic, astronomy, music, medicine and architecture. The first seven are the general educational subjects for the free man (*artes liberales*) which the ancient world gave to the middle ages as a school programme. The work probably dates from Varro's late years. At least partly surviving is the *De lingua Latina* (twenty-five books, of which we possess, with gaps, books 5–10). Books 5–25 were dedicated to Cicero, and therefore fall before the end of 43 B.C. Like Cicero, in his 'academic' works, Varro starts with the presentation of the opposite point of view, so as to refute it. For our knowledge of ancient Rome the *De lingua Latina* is invaluable. — Literature in the narrower meaning of the word are the *Logistorici*, the *Saturae Menippeae* and the three books on agriculture (*rerum rusticarum*). The *Logistorici* were short philosophical treatises on particular themes with examples from history; the main speaker was always a specially competent personality, just as Cicero let the aged censor Cato speak on old age and Laelius, famed as a friend of Scipio, on friendship. — The one hundred and fifty *Saturae Menippeae* were probably written between 81 B.C. and 67 B.C. Characteristic of this form is a mixture of verse and prose and the blending of the realistic-mimetic with the moralizing element. How strongly Varro is influenced here by the Greeks is shown by the large number of Greek and Greco-Latin titles. In one of these *saturae* Varro gave advice on banquets, *e.g.* about the number and type of guests, and the right sort of table-talk. Fragments of the *saturae* are numerous, but only a few can be reconstructed. We can still recognize satire on the struggle of the philosophical schools, scorn of the foreign cults in Rome, parodies of myths, but especially the contrast between 'ancient' and 'modern' Rome, which also plays a big role in Varro's works on cultural history. In *Sexagesis* a Roman sinks into a deep sleep as a ten-year-old boy to awaken after fifty years. The sixty-year-old finds himself no longer at home in his city; everything is so different from the good old times. Finally the troublesome and old-fashioned man is thrown from a bridge into the Tiber. Here, as in other satires, the author introduces himself. Stylistically Varro is indebted in the earlier satires especially to Lucilius, but also to dramatic forms, *e.g.* the mime. Like Lucilius he unhesitatingly mixes Greek and Latin (that this was customary in colloquial language is shown by Cicero's letters). In contrast to the Greek cynic Menippos (about 280 B.C.), the criticism of Varro takes its standards not so much from human nature as from Roman custom. Cicero makes him say of himself that he has copied Menippos, but did not translate him. — Varro wrote his three books *rerum rusticarum* when almost eighty years old (1 : agriculture, 2 : stock-farming, 3 : bird and fish breeding). This work survives nearly complete. Its cleverly handled dialogue form, its wit, and its often slightly archaic language have a certain charm.

Varro, who was Cicero's elder by ten years and outlived him by another fifteen, spans a bridge from Lucilius and Accius to the ascent of Vergil and Horace; but he was not, like Cicero, a focal point of the intellectual trends and cultural forces of his time. His Pythagorean leanings did not at any rate go as far as those of his (and Cicero's) friend P. Nigidius Figulus, who not only wrote on prophecy and astrology, but also practised occultism and clairvoyance. Side by side with a weakness for Pythagorean number symbolism there was in Varro the rationalism of the scientist. As a scholar he had taken in Greek culture in all its breadth, even if not in all its depth, and applied the methods of Greek research to subjects which for the Romans had a practical or at least a sentimental value. Yet too often he did not get beyond a collection of materials, nor can his pedantic classification conceal the lack of a genuine system. But he had brought together a treasure of knowledge and enriched it through his own antiquarian, literary and historical research; he also gave the West a programme of general education which in a certain sense is still valid today.

HISTORY AND BIOGRAPHY

Among the historians C. IULIUS CAESAR (100–44 B.C.) towers above the rest not only because of his powerful personality but also because of the unique nature of his historical work. To tell the story of Caesar's life would mean to write the history of his time. We are concerned here only with Caesar the writer. Natural talent, a liberal education and the convention of his social set led Caesar to literature in his early youth; he found time for it even in the midst of the most hectic activities of his later years. He wrote the two books *De analogia* (a defence of his linguistic purism) during his crossing of the Alps in 54 B.C.; on his way to Spain in 46 B.C. he wrote a poem *Iter* (presumably in imitation of Lucilius). The two books *Anticatones* (against the eulogies of Cicero and Brutus) belong to the pamphleteering literature of the political crisis. As an orator he was, according to Quintilian's judgement, almost Cicero's equal; Cicero himself praises not only Caesar's purity and elegance of speech but also the great impact of his delivery and appearance. In the fragments of Caesar's orations we find a style which differs completely from Cicero's; without falling into extremes, he still keeps much nearer to Atticism. The ancient world also knew collections of Caesar's letters; only the few which Cicero enclosed in his letters to Atticus are preserved.

Caesar did not take his literary activity quite seriously; for him it was partly a relaxation in leisure hours, partly a means of political propaganda. In this light we must see also the work which gives him a place in world literature: his *Commentarii rerum gestarum* — the seven books *De bello Gallico* and the three books *De bello civili*. They were not precisely 'propaganda' in the modern sense. The accounts of his Gallic victories are certainly meant to impress; he does try to represent his policy of conquest, for which he had no commission, as necessary security measures; but he addresses himself exclusively to the members of his own class. The books on the civil war were perhaps intended for a somewhat larger public. They are doubt-less meant as a self-justification; the senate and Pompey are blamed for the conflict. Yet, when all is said, both works are primarily the memoirs of a politician who would like to see *his* version of events on record: not history, but an official account. Caesar 'rearranged' his facts most cleverly; he has been accused, not quite unjustly, of misrepresentation. But rarely can a statement of his be proved to be factually untrue.

The principal sources of the *commentarii* are of course the reports of Caesar's officers and his own camp diaries; for the *Bellum Gallicum* also Caesar's official reports to the senate, the Roman equivalent of the reports of hellenistic generals to their sovereigns. The published *commentarii* of Caesar have their direct literary forerunners in the memoirs of Scaurus, Rutilius Rufus, Lutatius Catulus and Sulla, who also wanted to justify their own policy or strategy.

In his *commentarii* Caesar proves himself a master in the art of writing. Book I of the Gallic war still preserves more or less the form of a diary: the two campaigns of 58 B.C., against the

Helvetians and against Ariovistus, follow one upon the other and are not connected. On the other hand, in book 7 Caesar depicts the insurrection and the final defeat of Vercingetorix, without actually breaking his chosen framework, almost as a historical drama: here he even resorts to the device of direct speech, all the more effective for its sparing use. Vercingetorix is the only Gaul in Caesar's work who stands before us as a living person, be it only as a foil to Caesar's own greatness. Elements of literary historiography are also the geographical, ethnographical and technical digressions (building of the Rhine bridge; the Suevi; Britain; customs of the Gauls and Germans), whether they were composed by others under Caesar's eyes or put in by himself.

Caesar's style is unique. The purist principle (*tamquam scopulum ita fugias inauditum atque insolens verbum*, 'steer clear of an unheard and unusual word, as from the rock', as Gellius quotes from *De analogia*), which Caesar handled with some freedom in his orations, is here strictly adhered to, especially in the *Bellum Gallicum*; it is evident in every aspect — vocabulary, word forms, phraseology and construction. The *Bellum civile* is stylistically not quite so strict. That need not be intentional; Caesar wrote it in a hurry and may occasionally have only imperfectly recast in his own style the reports of his officers. No less remarkable than Caesar's language is his gift of combining vividness of presentation with conciseness. This stands out particularly in descriptions of landscape: structural, not picturesque, seen with the eyes of the strategist. Whoever has read in school the first book of the Gallic war and later comes to Besançon, will be reminded of Caesar's description of Vesontio (I, 38).

The most striking stylistic feature of the *commentarii* is that Caesar always speaks of himself in the third person. This is not inherent in the form of the *commentarius*. His accounts thus gain in clarity and detachment and give an impression of objectivity which could be achieved in no other way.

The gap between *Bellum Gallicum* 1–7 (58–52 B.C.) and *Bellum Civile* (49–48 B.C.) is filled by the eighth book *De Bello Gallico*. Its author is A. Hirtius, an officer of Caesar's general staff, who clearly had something to do with the preparation of the *commentarii* and in a large measure made the style of his general his own. Hirtius himself fell as consul at Mutina (43 B.C.). Perhaps he is also the author of the anonymous *Bellum Alexandrinum*, which is a sequel to the third book of Caesar's *Bellum Civile*. The continuation of the war (*Bellum Africum* and *Hispaniense*) is the work of officers who make little pretension to style; while the author of the *Bellum Africum* was at least an intelligent strategic observer, not even this can be said for the author of the *Bellum Hispaniense*.

Historical studies were pursued also by a friend of Cicero's, CORNELIUS NEPOS (about 99–24 B.C.), who came from Northern Italy. Catullus, who dedicated his poems to him, alludes to his *Chronica*, which is mentioned also by Gellius and other late authors. This chronicle recorded both Greek and Roman events; myths seem to have been treated as early history. Nepos is better known as a biographer. He wrote *inter alia* biographies of the elder Cato and of Cicero. His chief work *De viris illustribus* (at least sixteen books) contained short biographies of Romans and Greeks, arranged in groups like Varro's *Imagines*. The only book remaining is *De excellentibus ducibus exterarum gentium* and two biographies from the book *De historicis Latinis*. As a historian Nepos depended entirely on such derivative work as the hellenistic literature on 'Great men'; that his was not a critical mind has been justly remarked by the elder Pliny. He may be said to represent the average educated man of his time.

The most detailed and lively biography of Nepos is that of his and Cicero's friend T. POMPONIUS ATTICUS (109–32 B.C.). A banker and publisher on a large scale, he was also a highly educated man of wide interests. His favourite subject was family history. This is evident also in his principal work, the *Liber Annalis* (published in 47 B.C.), a city chronicle, which had room, besides politics, for family history, but also for literature. His chronology was based on Varro's.

A historian in the full meaning of the term was C. SALLUS-TIUS CRISPUS. Born in Sabine Amiternum in 86 B.C., he tried to make a political career as a *novus homo*. A follower of Caesar, he was quaestor under the Triumvirate (the date is uncertain) and tribune of the people in 52 B.C., a violent opponent of Milo and Cicero. His private life, no better (and perhaps no worse) than that of the Roman upper class which he later so harshly criticized, was taken as a pretext to expel the partisan of Caesar from the senate. Caesar rehabilitated him (47 B.C.); after his praetorship (46 B.C.) he held the province of Africa with the title of a proconsul. He must have filled his coffers there; his acquittal from a charge of extortion, which as usual followed his year of office, shows only that he had powerful influence. His house and the famous *horti Sallustiani* on the present Monte Pincio were later the property and occasional residence of Roman Emperors. Sallust died in 35 B.C.

The historical works of Sallust were all written in the last decade of his life, after Caesar's death; he was disgusted with politics, especially with Antony and his minions in the senate. His historical work is as it were an epilogue on the years through which he had lived. But beyond this Sallust wanted to interpret history and make its study fruitful. With this goal in view he justified the claim of the historian (first reservedly, later with conviction) to enjoy equal esteem with the active politician. A historian who so conceives his task cannot write annals; he will look about for a subject which to him and others reveals the meaning of history. Sallust wrote two monographs, one on the Catilinarian conspiracy, the other on the war with Jugurtha; the choice of subject is characteristic. Even his last work, the *Historiae*, which he carried down to the year 67 B.C., was similar in artistic form to its predecessors.

Among Roman historians Sallust has a special place. Historical writing is to him first and foremost an art. Yet he is just as far removed from the rhetorical historiography of hellenism, which comes from the school of Isocrates, as from the historical romance of the Alexander legend; on the other hand he is not a pragmatic historian like Polybius or his Roman follower Sempronius Asellio. He places himself consciously and directly in the tradition of Thucydides. His speeches, letters and digressions are not, as in hellenism, mere ornaments; as with Thucydides they serve the purpose of historical interpretation. But while Thucydides carefully ascertained and critically tested his facts, Sallust judges history dogmatically. In facts as such he has no direct and genuine interest; he is not even consistently accurate in reporting them. Protestations of truthfulness (in regard to contemporary events) may be conventional, but he can hardly ever be caught at a deliberate falsification of history. He himself claims only the objectivity possible to him (*quam verissume potero*, 'as accurately as I can'). Not only has he a preconceived picture of the powers at work in history; he also writes as a party man.

The model of a philosophical historian at the time was Posidonius, and Sallust might easily have come under his influence. Yet as far as we can see, he owes him little apart from factual details. He knew his Plato, and even saw his own withdrawal from politics in the light of Plato's seventh letter, but his political philosophy is not platonic. Still less is he a stoic. Even more strongly than Cicero he believes in the citizen's duty to live an active life. While in Cicero the politician and the philosopher do not always see eye to eye, *e.g.* in the concept of *virtus* or in the valuation of fame, for Sallust fame is the end and motive of all action. This fame, to be sure, must be won through *virtus*; not the *virtus* of the philosophers, but that of the unreflecting 'wise men', with whom Sallust (like Cicero in his *Laelius*) identified the Romans of the old times: a practical virtue whose nature is determined by tradition, not by theoretical speculation. This *virtus* had made Rome great; ambition, greed for power, wealth and luxury are to blame for her decline.

Sallust's mastery of the historiographer's art is worthy of our admiration. The architecture of his monographs, which grows organically from the author's concept of his subject, the tension which is subtly created and is maintained to the end, his characterizations, convincing despite their simple psychology, not least the author's language, impressive in its archaic roughness, all these qualities exercise, today as in antiquity, their power on the reader. Sallust wrote purposely an archaic Latin, especially in some of the speeches, a Latin which is modelled on that of the censor Cato and the early historians, but also on the epic style of Ennius. Contemporaries, *e.g.* Asinius Pollio, took offence at the boldness and obscurity of his diction; Livy, too, criticized Sallust's style. Tacitus on the other hand calls Sallust *rerum Romanorum florentissimus auctor* ('the finest flower of Roman historians') and is himself very much under his influence stylistically.

POETRY

The literary mime. — After Matius in Sulla's time had created an art-form of mime on the Greek model (which, however, was not meant for the stage), the mime now succeeded *palliata*, *togata* and *atellana*, as a literary comedy. The most important mime writers were the knight D. LABERIUS and the freedman PUBLILIUS SYRUS. Of Laberius numerous titles are known to us, in which we recognize on the one hand the themes of the *palliata* (*Colax, Hecyra, Phasma*), on the other those of the *togata* and *atellana* (*Augur, Fullo, Staminariae, Nuptiae, Gemelli, Compitalia, Saturnalia*). Publilius was famous as an actor who loved to improvise. Of his mimes only two titles and a few fragments are quoted.

D. Laberius, as one would expect from his rank, proves himself a man of culture. In the surviving fragments of his mimes we find many allusions to philosophy: to the cynics, Democritus, and the teachings of the Pythagoreans. He also not infrequently alluded to politics, and especially made fun of Caesar.

The dictator revenged himself by inviting the sixty-year-old Laberius to take part, at his triumphal games in 46 B.C., in a contest of improvised mimes to which Caesar's favourite, Publilius Syrus, had challenged his rivals. This meant for Laberius, who could not refuse Caesar's invitation, public appearance as a *mimus* and with it the loss of his social status. In the surviving prologue Laberius yields with noble resignation to his fate. In the mime itself, of which a few lines are quoted, there were not only attacks on his rival (Laberius played the part of a slave Syrus), but also on the dictatorship of Caesar. The latter as arbitrator gave the prize to Publilius, but returned to Laberius his ring, the emblem of equestrian rank. Laberius died in Puteoli at the beginning of 43 B.C. His mimes were popular despite the demands they made on their public; they may have owed this partly to their action (no longer known to us), but certainly also to their lively, popular and often, as the genre required, rather gross language.

When Laberius died, Publilius Syrus was at the height of his fame. Unfortunately it is even more difficult to get an idea of the mimes of Syrus than of those of Laberius. The one longer fragment from an unnamed mime by Publilius Syrus, which Petronius makes his Trimalchio quote, belongs to the familiar commonplaces against table-luxury and seductive female dress. There was a collection of his sayings (*sententiae*) as early as the first century A.D.; they were used as a school-book. Of the seven hundred or so sayings, mostly in six-foot iambics, only few are likely to be genuine.

Lucretius.— T. Lucretius Carus seems as strange a figure in his own times as his poem is unique in all Roman literature. Not only did he, as a convinced epicurean, keep away from politics as did many others; even as a poet, Lucretius is difficult to imagine in a social context. To expound the teachings of Epicurus, especially his physics, in a poem was a double venture: the idea of a philosophical poem was absurd to the orthodox epicurean, and its execution had to struggle with almost insoluble aesthetic problems. Theoretical prejudice against poetry had little power over Lucretius, a born poet, who might not have become an epicurean until his mature years; and though he had thoroughly imbibed Epicurus's teaching, there is no trace in his work of the epicurean temperament. Inclined by nature to melancholy, he constantly felt the urge to reassure himself of the liberation which he owed to Epicurus; hence his impulse to proclaim it with the fervour of a missionary. His inspiration let him see even in that dry material the germ of a poem, and his art made of it a masterpiece, *De rerum natura*, one of the few didactic poems of world literature to have a lasting appeal.

Lucretius, a member of the *gens Lucretia* probably by birth-right, and not as a client, according to Jerome born in 96 B.C. or 95 B.C., was alleged to have gone mad through taking a love potion and in this condition, not yet forty-four years old (probably in 53 B.C.), to have committed suicide; in the lucid spells of his mental illness, so the account goes on, he wrote his epic, which Cicero afterwards emended. This story, however, is not very credible as a whole or either in all its details.

In the six books *De rerum natura* Lucretius expounds the physics, psychology and theory of culture of Epicurus; the epicurean ethics are treated but incidentally. Books 1 and 2 contain the doctrine of the atoms, 3 and 4 treat of the life-principle (*anima*) and spirit (*animus*), 5 and 6 of the world and its phenomena, heavenly and earthly, including the origins and development of human culture. In books 1, 2 and 5, which many scholars regard as the earliest, Lucretius addresses C. Memmius, who was then (57 B.C.) pro-praetor in Bithynia; he wants to win him to the teaching of Epicurus, which he himself has experienced as a spiritual liberation. The manner in which Lucretius speaks to Memmius is not suggestive of social inequality.

The sources of Lucretius were above all the writings of Epicurus himself. His artistic model, in many ways, was the poem *Peri physeos* ('about nature') of the Sicilian Empedocles (about 450 B.C.). The connexion can be seen not only in the subject matter but also in the structure, form and spirit of the poem.

Lucretius himself is quite explicit as regards his didactic purpose: as a disciple of Epicurus he wants to free people from religion, that is (for him) from fear of gods and death, by making them realize that everything is natural and transitory. The way towards this goal leads through the difficult and unattractive study of epicurean physics. This he sweetens for Memmius with his verse, as the doctor spreads the rim of the medicine cup with honey. The impulse to write the poem, however, comes to him from the Muses. He is the first to venture on this untrodden path, to make the *ratio* of Epicurus the subject of a *carmen*. As Sallust hoped that his historical writing would make him deservedly famous, so a similar hope animated the apostle of a philosophy of seclusion. With Epicurus, the pleasure-principle is realized in the simple life, free from passion and other disturbances of one's peace of mind, in man's delight in nature, in reasonable and moderate sensual pleasure, and in the study of the nature of things, which puts an end to all irrational fear. The conqueror of religion becomes for Lucretius the founder of a new, a rational religion, a saviour, in fact almost a god. This Roman atheist gives proof of his keen religious sense also in his description of religious ceremonies; having warmed up, *malgré lui*, to his subject, it is not without some effort that he finds back to his professed rationalism.

Lucretius often breaks into pure, non-didactic poetry. Especially elevated are the prologues to the several books: the prayer to Venus which inspired Botticelli's 'Primavera', and the enthusiastic praise of Epicurus; so is also the long passage on the development of human culture, which closes book 5. Some descriptions which relieve the didacticism have a strong human appeal: descriptions of Nature in her charm and her terror, descriptions of human existence in its friendly and fearful aspects, of the happiness of family life, of love and passion or of the great plague of Athens. But even in minor details Lucretius makes the abstract doctrine come to life.

Stylistically, Lucretius stands between the old and the new poetry: beside imitations of Ennius there are points of contact with the 'new' poetry of young Cicero, and there is also the typically hellenistic description of the Cybele procession. Rhetorical elements are very consciously applied, especially accumulated alliteration. The frequent repetition of formulae and shorter or longer groups of lines may be partly explained by the scientific nature of the subject (many repeated verses are translations or periphrases of sentences of Epicurus), partly by the unfinished form of the poem, partly, as perhaps also in the case of Empedocles, as an element of epic tradition.

The work of Lucretius was known to the end of antiquity, and was studied and copied also in Carolingian times; in the late middle ages it was forgotten and not discovered again till the Renaissance. Since then Lucretius has never ceased to be with us; now attacked as an atheist, now celebrated as an enlightener, but above all, transcending the dispute about his *Weltanschauung*, as a great European poet.

The New Poets.— Under this name we are used to refer to a number of poets who form a group, if not exactly a school. They represent a generation: their childhood or early youth falls under Sulla's dictatorship, the death of most of them between Pharsalus and Actium (48–31 B.C.). It is symptomatic that several hailed from Gallia Transpadana. What links these poets together is their dislikes rather than any positive goals. Their turning away from Ennius is a renunciation of the earlier Roman poetry in both spirit and form. They want to write poetry like the Greeks: more precisely, like the Alexandrians. It is *l'art pour l'art*: partly out-of-the-way material treated with recondite erudition, partly a striving for the perfect form in conveying even the most fleeting personal experience; both aiming at the absolute perfection of formal art, for which every sacrifice of time and effort was made : Cinna actually worked at his *Zmyrna* for nine years (as Horace later recommended to the budding poet). It is not a mere coincidence that just at this time — perhaps through Cinna's friend Parthenios, who came to Rome from Bithynia between 73 and 66 B.C. — the hellenistic custom of individual wedding- and mourning-poems was introduced. The epigram and the lyric forms, known already from Lutatius, Catulus and Laevius, were cultivated with a new zeal and a refined technique. Greek words and word-forms were in vogue for the sake of their sound, the Greek letters y and z were given their place in the Latin alphabet, and Greek constructions were imitated ; in the hexameter the soft and typically Alexandrian double spondee was sought after as a verse-ending. The poets and their audience became sensitive to speech- and verse-melody, and valued careful choice of words and studied patterns of word-order. In contrast to the Alexandrians as well as to the Augustans, their aestheticism did not prevent them from participation in public life : Calvus and Cornificius were celebrated as forensic orators (Atticists) ; Cornificius and Helvius Cinna were also politically active as followers of Caesar ; Catullus, Calvus, and others wrote political poems. They do not all stand in the same camp ; Furius Bibaculus even changed from an opponent of Caesar to his panegyrist.

The head and 'teacher' of the New Poets was P. VALERIUS CATO. Having forfeited his family inheritance in the Sullan proscriptions, he earned his living as a *grammaticus*, but retained his pride. His lessons were treasured. He wrote an *indignatio* of personal content (in verse), an epyllion (*Diana* or *Dictynna*), and a mythological-erotic poem *Lydia*. C. LICINIUS CALVUS (82–47 B.C.) was even more versatile. Besides a lament on his wife and an epithalamium he wrote political verse against Pompey and Caesar, but also love poems and an epyllion, *Io*, modelled, it seems, on both Callimachus and the *Prometheus* of Aeschylus. C. HELVIUS CINNA (a friend of Catullus and with him in the *cohors praetoria* of Memmius, 57 B.C., murdered in

44 B.C. in the tumult at Caesar's funeral) had come very much under the influence of Parthenios, as may be seen in his choosing *Zmyrna* as his heroine. The incest motive (love of father and daughter) would have appealed to him because of its unusual possibilities of psychological treatment. He also wrote a farewell poem for the young Asinius Pollio, on his departure for Greece; this form of occasional poetry soon became popular. Only an epigram, imitative of Callimachus, survives complete. To this generation also belongs M. FURIUS BIBACULUS of Cremona. In his early verse he attacked Caesar, who, however, forgave him; later he glorified Caesar's success in Gaul in an epic *Annales belli Gallici*. To write an annalistic epic was a renunciation of his artistic past. A proof of the lighter side of his art are the gently mocking lines on the revered Valerius Cato. CICERO too in his early poetry, in the *Aratea* and even more so in such poetic attempts as *Halcyones*, appeared as a New Poet; his return to the old tradition, in his own poetry as in his literary judgement, would seem to have had principally patriotic and moralistic motives: for him poetry is not aesthetic play, but (as he affirms in the oration *pro Archia*) serious and responsible work for the benefit of the community. P. TERENTIUS VARRO (82–37 B.C.), called Atacinus after the river Atax in his native Provence, went the opposite way. After writing an epic in Ennian style about 55 B.C. (*Bellum Sequanicum*, probably Caesar's war against Ariovistus), he was later attracted by the Alexandrians. His chief work, unfortunately lost, is the *Argonautae* (after Apollonios); from some fragments we can still see that occasionally he surpassed the original, especially in description of nature. Of other poets like C. Memmius, Q. Cornificius, and his sister Cornificia we know too little to judge them. There were also numerous amateurs who by no means lacked talent; to write verse had become a fashion in high society.

Of all the New Poetry only the poems of C. VALERIUS CATULLUS survive, thanks perhaps to the local patriotism of his native city, Verona. There Catullus was born in about 84 B.C. His father was a personal friend of Caesar's, who liked to stay at his home when he came to the province. The son studied in Rome and, apart from occasional visits to his home, spent most of his life there. He moved in the best society, but felt most at ease in the company of his country-fellows from Transpadana, Cornelius Nepos and the New Poets, especially Calvus and Cinna. Like Calvus, Catullus attacked the Triumviri and their followers; his special target was an officer named Mamurra, who had used Caesar's favour to enrich himself on his campaigns and who (which Catullus took even more amiss) proved his rival with the ladies. Catullus had connexions also with Hortensius. In one poem he thanks Cicero (in an elevated tone, which sounds slightly ironical) for some favour.

Catullus showed as little inclination for public office as for business; he was sufficiently well-off to live as he pleased. He loved *otium*, he gave himself heart and soul to social life, to the company of his friends, to love, but above all to poetry. His datable poems fall between 60 B.C. and 55/54 B.C. What raises Catullus above the poets of his generation is the power and depth of his experience. This gift proved his fate in his love for Clodia, sister of the tribune P. Clodius Pulcher and wife of Q. Caecilius Metellus Celer, the 'Lesbia' of his poems. Her beauty and culture were as famous as her conduct (of which Cicero gives a decidedly malicious picture in *pro Caelio*) was notorious. In the Lesbia poems we experience with the intensely passionate poet the happiness and the torments of this love, until the final break and melancholy memory. His art even heightens the directness of the experience. In the year 57/56 B.C. we find Catullus in the *cohors praetoria* of Memmius in Bithynia and on a visit to the grave of his beloved brother in the Troad. Perhaps he hoped to forget Clodia, perhaps he meant to improve his finances, perhaps he was now thinking of a political career. Whatever it may have been, it came to nothing; about 54 B.C. Catullus died, only thirty years old.

The work of Catullus forms a collection of one hundred and sixteen poems: the first part consists of short poems in various metres ('bagatelles' — they are as perfect works of art as are Chopin's musical miniatures), the second of longer 'learned' poems, the last of epigrams in elegiac couplets. The collection is dedicated to Cornelius Nepos. Separately there survives a Priapeum, a poem on Priapos, the lascivious god who protected gardens. As in the volumes of poems by the Augustans (Vergil's eclogues, the love elegies, the odes of Horace), the poems are arranged on a formal and aesthetic principle, not chronologically.

In Catullus all the characteristic themes of the New Poets are united: love, the experience of friendship, pictures of nature, political lampoons and private satire, wedding songs, and laments. The directness of the lyrical poems and the epigrams is unique; no less personal than the Lesbia poems, for example, is the mischievous distich on Caesar. Catullus is also a master in the Italic art of lampooning; if his vocabulary is rich in the tenderest and most ardent (also the most outspoken) words of the language of love, it is inexhaustible when it comes to the coarse and filthy. Hatred and love, which made him miserable, were stronger than he; only in his art could he free himself from both.

A few poems are in a group by themselves, quiet and serene, as for example the dedication to the Dioscuri of his worn-out boat, or the greeting to Sirmio on Lake Garda; here too we might put the *ave atque vale* ('hail and farewell') to his dead brother, a poem whose quiet sadness contrasts so impressively with the passionate grief of the Allius elegy.

The longer poems of the middle section show us Catullus as *poeta doctus*. The miniature epic on the wedding of Peleus and Thetis has two 'insets': the description of the precious carpet with the story of Theseus and Ariadne (50–264) and the song of the Parcae with its twelve-times-recurring refrain (323–81). Mere description has, however, changed here to the lively telling of a story within the story: a contrast of fortunate and unfor-

tunate love, faithfulness and betrayal. No particular model has
so far been discovered; perhaps Catullus freely employed
Alexandrian themes, motifs and techniques and in the spirit of
his models created something of his own. The poem has been
interpreted even as an 'objectivation' of his love for Lesbia.
Learning is not more in evidence than fashion demanded; it did
not interest Catullus for its own sake. More of a learned study
is his translation of Callimachus's 'Berenice's lock', whose
original has become known partly from a papyrus. Catullus
dedicated this attempt to Hortensius. The Attis poem, written
in the rare and difficult galliambic metre, is also an imitation of
Callimachus. It impresses us not only as a *tour de force*, but also
as a poem: the description of the oriental orgiastic rites in the
first part contrasts effectively with the complaint of the castrated
Attis in the second. The group opens with two epithalamia;
the first, written for the wedding of Manlius Torquatus with
Vinia Aurunculeia, is a synthesis of Roman *fescennini* with
traditions of Greek style.

The last of the big poems is the elegy to Allius (c. 68). The
friend in his *chagrin d'amour* has asked Catullus to write for
him a poetical consolation. Catullus, though mourning over
the loss of his brother and his beloved, also without the books
which he needs for a scholarly poem, still wants to oblige his
friend, in whose house he has so often been allowed to meet
Lesbia. He reminds him of the days of his own blissful love,
which were short like those of Laodamia; she lost her Protesilaos
at Troy, and there, in the Troad, his brother too, from whose
grave he has just come home, is buried. That is the centre of the
poem; from here his thoughts turn back to the beginning, but
at the end stands a farewell greeting — not to Allius, but to
Lesbia. This poem is an anticipation of the subjective love
elegy, one of the most original creations of Roman literature.
In the same direction point some of Catullus's epigrams, which
have been appropriately described as short elegies, especially the
moving epilogue on his love for Lesbia, which ends in a prayer.

Catullus also introduced into Roman poetry a new lyrical form: the sapphic stanza. For Lesbia he translated a famous poem of Sappho; with pointed bitterness he chose the same stanza for her final rejection. The pseudonym of Lesbia[1] and the Lesbic stanza of the poem would seem to be related: what brought Clodia and Catullus together might well have been their love of the great poetess of Lesbos. Thus perhaps something quite personal led Catullus to a province of Greek poetry into which so far no Roman had ventured: the Aeolian lyric. An Aeolian stanza was used by Catullus also in the Diana hymn and the wedding song. Catullus was a pioneer; it was Horace who finally conquered the Aeolian song for the Romans.

[1] Lesbia is metrically equivalent to Clodia : such pseudonyms were later used by the elegiac poets.

4. The Augustan Era

43 B.C.–A.D. 14

LIFE AND LETTERS

THE murder of Caesar was followed by a new wave of civil wars and years of agonizing political tension. People breathed freely again when the victory at Actium (2nd September, 31 B.C.) gave C. Octavius, grand-nephew and adopted son of Caesar, a free hand for the pacification and reorganization of the state. The price was high: loss of republican freedom. At first, however, there prevailed a feeling of happiness and enthusiastic gratitude. Octavian had brought peace to a generation born in the civil wars; he restored tranquillity, security and prosperity to a world which had seen itself already on the edge of an abyss; by his victory over Cleopatra he had annexed the last great hellenistic kingdom, the wonderland of Egypt with its treasures, to the Roman Empire. The man who had achieved all this appeared as a saviour; the senate gave him the honorary title of Augustus, 'the illustrious', which he added henceforth to his name.

The reforms of Augustus were not limited to measures necessary for the military, administrative and economic consolidation of the empire; these were to be based on a spiritual and ethical renewal of the citizen body. The Romans were to learn to maintain the traditions of their great past in the spirit of a new era. This task fell above all to literature. Under Augustus Rome, for the first and last time, became the literary and artistic centre of the ancient world.

The Augustan age saw the zenith, if not of Roman literature in general, at any rate of Roman poetry. This poetry is not easy to approach for the modern reader, to whom its formalism and its character as court poetry are unlikely to appeal. In both respects, however, it resembles other great poetry: the Alexandrian, the poetry of the Italian Renaissance, the classical drama of France.

Striving after perfect form need not be at the expense of poetic substance. The Romans, like the Latin peoples of later times, attached great importance to form. The Augustan poets were doubly encumbered by tradition with Roman formality and Alexandrian artificiality. Genuine experience is there for anyone who is able to feel it, but it is controlled and restrained as was in keeping with the new spirit. In contrast to this, there is an undercurrent of strong sensuality, *e.g.* in a few of Horace's epodes and satires, but especially in the love elegy. Ovid's *Art of Love* is the radical denial of the moral revival which Augustus wanted; he never forgave the poet.

That we have to do with court poetry is only partly true. Augustus knew what he was doing when he inspired and patronized literature. The temple of Apollo on the Palatine, opened by Augustus in 28 B.C., which contained an important public library, had as its cult image the Apollo Citharodos of Scopas. Apollo, lord of the muses, god of light and order, conqueror of the dragon Python, became the symbol of Augustus, and the divine protector of his house. Men who had his confidence like Maecenas, who was to become proverbial, but also many who stood a little apart like M. Valerius Messala, were centres of literary circles. One of the most independent among literary men of the period, C. Asinius Pollio (he had, *e.g.* in 39 B.C., founded a public library after the hellenistic pattern, the first in Rome), had connexions not only with Cicero, Catullus and Cinna, but also with Cornelius Gallus, the young Vergil and Horace, although one cannot speak here of a circle.

'Court poetry', of course, implies more: a poetry for the glorification of the ruler, an instrument in the service of his interests. Was the Augustan literature 'inspired' by Augustus?

In the genuine meaning of the word, certainly; in the journal-istic, propagandist sense, certainly not. Maecenas was not merely the head of a propaganda bureau. Vergil, Horace and others sincerely believed in Augustus's mission; they saw in him not only the saviour of the state, but also the embodiment of the ideas which shaped their time. Augustus, on his part, knew very well the political value of a great literature, but he also saw that in order to serve him as he wished it must be genuine, and therefore free in its own sphere. Nothing proves this attitude better than the fact that one poet after the other could decline without fear the insinuated invitation to glorify Augustus directly; Horace even rejected an honourable office at court without losing the emperor's favour.

A literature which so consciously, and almost officially, voiced the thoughts and feelings of the ruling people of the time would rise to a prominence and dignity hitherto unknown. The poet now, irrespective of his social rank, merely by virtue of his vocation — he liked to call himself *Vates* ('seer') — held a place in the life of the nation that no Roman author ever before had held. Cicero, who for us represents his time most perfectly, still felt the need for excusing his literary work with the involun-tary leisure imposed on him by the political situation; Horace, the son of a freedman, considered his odes worthy of the triumph-ant generals' laurels, and that was neither meant as a presumption nor was it so understood. The danger that this 'imperial poetry' might become too representative was, however, not always avoided.

Only one of the great Augustans stands apart: the latest, Ovid. On the day of Actium he was not yet twelve years old; he belonged to a new generation who knew of the civil war only from hearsay and took the blessings of peace for granted. The spiritual and moral powers from which it had grown meant nothing to him; poetry was to him an urge and an end in itself. On the other hand he is the only poet of rank in whom one finds overt flattery. But Augustus was not easily deceived.

Poets now turned away from the Alexandrians: their models were Homer and Hesiod, Archilochus, Mimnermus, Alcaeus and (experimentally, in the later work of Horace) Pindar. We see this change most clearly in the work of Vergil: from bagatelles in the style of Catullus, through the bucolic poetry of Theocritus, to works in which he tries to be a Roman Hesiod and Homer. In the process, the Alexandrian bucolic, the Ionic iambus and the Aeolian lyric became Roman.

A heritage of the New Poets was the care bestowed on composition. This is true not only of the epic and of cycles of stories (*Aeneid, Metamorphoses*) but also of the bucolic and lyric poetry, of satire and elegy: the individual poems are arranged with a view to giving artistic unity to the entire book.

In general Augustan poetry may be likened to the sculpture and architecture of its time. It is the golden mean between extremes, a 'mean' in the Aristotelian sense. It blends severity with charm, simplicity with dignity, experience with objectivity, attention to detail with due regard for the broad outline.

Augustan prose, of which little is known apart from Livy, falls behind poetry. The climax of Latin prose had already been reached with Cicero. The power that shaped it had been free speech, for which there was less and less room under the principate. Cicero had enriched oratory by philosophy and science. These interests too, which had little support in the curricula of the schools, were on the wane. The study of philosophy was limited almost completely to the mere adoption of an often eclectic system. An exception were the two Sextii (father and son), who rigorously followed the cynics and early stoics.

In its more conventional forms, however, philosophy had a wider appeal: men of such different nature as Pollio, Vergil, Horace, Vitruvius and Livy turned towards it. But of a need to understand the world and man scientifically, there is no evidence.

The most important scientific achievement of the time was

the world map, which the general of Augustus, M. Vipsanius Agrippa, caused to be designed. It was of course a work of applied science, of practical value; its public exhibition on the Field of Mars was an effective piece of propaganda. Dedicated to Augustus are the ten books *De architectura* of VITRUVIUS POLLIO. Stylistically no masterpiece — the language wavers between affectation and artlessness — this handbook is of great value for its contents. The author, who was a military engineer under Caesar, is both expert and well-read in his subject. His treatise is also an act of homage to the *princeps*, who 'found Rome as a city of bricks and left it as a city of marble'. The extensive work of M. VERRIUS FLACCUS, which survives only in extracts, is much more than its title, *De significatu verborum* ('About the meanings of words'), would suggest: it is a historical and antiquarian encyclopaedia of ancient Rome. A work of profound scholarship, it follows Augustus's desire to raise the Roman past to new life. Here too belong the *Libri rerum rusticarum* of the eighty-year-old Varro, whose chronological vicinity to Vergil's *Georgics* is no accident: the cultivation of the soil of Italy, laid waste in the civil war, was a matter of life and death for people and government.

Legal science underwent a fundamental change. The giving of legal opinions, which had hitherto been a matter of personal trust, from now on required the authority of the *princeps*. This led to the formation of a jurist class, and soon there were law schools, opposed to each other's teaching. The two main schools, formed under the Claudians, go back to the two most renowned jurists of the Augustan era, the uncompromising M. Antistius Labeo, a man of extensive education and wide interests, and the accommodating C. Ateius Capito, preferred by the *princeps*, a connoisseur of sacred law, who was commissioned to work out the ritual for the celebration of the *saeculum* in 17 B.C.

It was in the field of oratory that the new regime made itself most heavily felt. The people's assemblies became more and more an empty form without political significance; the senate lapsed into ever greater dependence on the *princeps*; the majority of important legal cases were taken away from the jury-courts and came before the *princeps* and a senatorial commission. Messala and Pollio, who had been active as orators in the days of the republic, withdrew into the private sphere of literature. One of the last true orators, CASSIUS SEVERUS, fell out of favour on account of his aggressiveness. The orator and historian T. LABIENUS made no secret of his republican convictions; his books were burned by order of the senate, whereupon the author (about A.D. 12) committed suicide. In a recitation from his historical work even he found it necessary to suppress many passages, with the remark that they were not to be read until after his death.

The enjoyment of oratory as an art, however, did not die out. It withdrew from the forum and was now for the first time an 'art' in the narrower sense. The teachers of rhetoric, who soon controlled higher education completely, gave not only model declamations for their pupils, but also public demonstrations of their virtuosity, and so prepared the way for the professional 'wandering orators' of later times. What for Cicero had been a stimulating pastime now became a profession. Labienus still found public declamation beneath his dignity and Cassius Severus, who occasionally brought himself to doing it, did not take it seriously enough to shine in it. Among the older generation the foremost school orators were the Spaniard M. PORCIUS LATRO and the Asiatic Greek ARELLIUS FUSCUS. Latro, despite his hoarse voice, was among his contemporaries the unequalled master of his art and the idol of his pupils; Fuscus recited more in Greek than in Latin, and led Asianism in Rome to a new climax. Our most important source for the rhetoric under Augustus and Tiberius is a work of the elder L. ANNAEUS SENECA from Cordoba, the father of the philosopher: *Oratorum et rhetorum sententiae, divisiones, colores*, which he wrote for his sons in his old age (about 54 B.C.–A.D. 39?) from his unusually sound memory. The work comprises ten books of *controversiae* (fictitious law cases) and one book of *suasoriae* (exposés of fictitious situations). According to the testimony of his son, Seneca was also a writer of *Historiae*.

Besides the public declamation of the orator there was the literary recitation. It developed from the custom, familiar to the Greeks and Romans, of reading a work in a circle of discriminating friends before it was published. Pollio, who even after his retreat from public life could not do without an audience, was the first person to send out invitations to such readings; soon readings before invited guests or before a wider audience became the fashion. Originally, it would seem, recitations were confined to reading from one's own works; later there were also recitations from earlier literature.

Leading men continued to try their hand at literature in the tradition of the republican *nobiles*. Augustus himself wrote among other things *hortationes ad philosophiam*, an autobiographical work, *fescennini* and a tragedy *Ajax*, which, however, he destroyed. His *Res gestae* and statistics of the empire (*Breviarium totius imperii*) were of an official nature. An unusual figure is C. MAECENAS (died 8 B.C.). Clever and effeminate, vain, yet without ambition, and proud of his Etruscan ancestry, he led a life of cultured leisure in the spirit of Epicurus, only occasionally interrupted by diplomatic missions and the discharge of special duties with which Augustus entrusted him from time to time. Himself only a dilettante in poetry, and not even a good one, he did possess a sure instinct for the poetic gifts of others. To his circle belonged almost all the great poets of the time: Vergil, Varius, Horace, Domitius Marsus; even Propertius tried to win his favour. The literary ambitions of C. ASINIUS POLLIO must be taken much more seriously. Of his tragedies, in the style of Pacuvius and Accius, Vergil and Horace speak with respect; even Tacitus still knew them. Pollio's chief work was *Historiae* in seventeen books, a history of the civil war from the first Triumvirate (60 B.C.) to (perhaps) the battle of Philippi (42 B.C.) or even to his own consulate

(40 B.C.); he intentionally did not go on beyond that. About Pollio as an orator the younger Seneca passes a harsh, Quintilian a carefully reserved, judgement. Pollio himself, on the other hand, was anything but reserved in his criticism of the style of his contemporaries, from Cicero to Livy. The literary activity of M. VALERIUS MESSALA, from the time when he no longer appeared as an orator, consisted primarily of science, philosophy and antiquarianism. He also wrote memoirs in Greek.

THE MASTERS

P. VERGILIUS MARO

Vergil was born near Mantua on 15th October 70 B.C., as the son of Vergilius Maro and Magia Polla. His father's name was Etruscan, his mother's (perhaps) Oscan; that he was a Celt is not demonstrable. Father and son probably held Roman citizenship. He grew up in simple surroundings with two brothers who died before him. He had his first lessons in Cremona where he seems to have lived with his parents. After putting on the toga of manhood on his fifteenth birthday, he studied, as was customary, rhetoric: first in Milan, then in Rome. Yet he made only one appearance as an orator, and that without success. Much more interesting to him was philosophy, and also mathematics and medicine. He attached himself to the circle of the epicurean Siro in Naples, of whom Cicero speaks approvingly on several occasions. A country house of Siro became at one time an asylum for Vergil's family. Vergil was already grown up when his father died. His mother married again and had one son of her second marriage, Valerius Proculus.

When in 41 B.C. land was expropriated in Transpadana to settle the veterans of Philippi, Vergil's family estate shared the fate of confiscation. Asinius Pollio, who recognized Vergil's poetic talent, obtained for him either restitution or compensation. He also introduced the young poet to Octavian.

In those years (42–39 B.C.) the *Eclogues* were written, which

established Vergil's fame as a poet; they were even recited in
the theatre. Besides homage to Pollio and their mutual friend,
Cornelius Gallus, there are compliments to Vergil's life-long
friend Alfenus Varus from Cremona, and to Helvius Cinna.

In his next work, the *Georgics*, Vergil took up a suggestion
from Maecenas, to whose circle he now belonged. Whatever
Maecenas's motive was, the subject must have been very attractive to Vergil, a nature-lover, who never became a city man.
Work on the poem lasted seven years. Vergil lived mostly in
the south, in Sicily and Campania, especially in Naples. In
Rome, where Maecenas had given him a house on the Esquiline,
he did not feel at home; when he was recognized and honoured
in the street, he fled, embarrassed, into the nearest building.
While working on the *Georgics*, Vergil used to dictate in the
morning a large number of lines which during the day he reduced to a few; he compared himself to a mother bear licking
her uncouth cubs into shape. The work was ready when in
29 B.C. Octavian came home from the East; he had it read to
him during a stay in Atella; Vergil and Maecenas recited it in
turn.

His ever-increasing fame — once when he visited the theatre
the audience rose in his honour as it would do for Augustus —
seems to have meant very little to Vergil. The dark-com-
plexioned man with the peasant face and the faltering speech
was happy only in the most intimate circle of friends. To this
circle belonged, beside his fellow countryman Alfenus Varus,
L. Varius, Plotius Tucca, Cornelius Gallus and, not least, Horace,
whom he himself had recommended to Maecenas.

Soon after the completion of the *Georgics*, Vergil started his
greatest work, the *Aeneid*, the new epic of the Roman people.
Augustus took an active interest in it. From his Cantabrian
campaigns (27–25 B.C.) he wrote to the poet, demanding that
he should send him as soon as possible a sketch of the work or
some finished part. The expectations of Rome's men of letters
were voiced enthusiastically by Propertius, who announced the

E

Aeneid in about 26 B.C. But the work progressed slowly. Vergil had first divided the material into twelve books, and worked out details as the spirit would move him. He left half-lines so as not to hinder the flow of inspiration (at a recitation before friends he once completed two half-lines on the spur of the moment); other lines he used only as 'supports' (*tibicines*), in whose place he would later put the true columns. Not until some time after Augustus's return from the war did Vergil present three finished books (2, 4 and 6) to him and his sister Octavia; the lines on her son, the recently deceased Marcellus, heir-presumptive to the throne (book VI, 860 ff.), so moved her that she swooned.

In eleven years the work had come near completion; but Vergil, far from being satisfied with it, decided to travel to Greece and Asia Minor in order to follow his hero step by step while putting the finishing touches to his poem. However, when he arrived at Athens and there met Augustus on his way home from the East, he was persuaded to return with the emperor. On visiting the city of Megara in stifling heat the poet was seized by a fever. The journey only made his condition worse. He died in Brundisium, a few days after landing, on 21 September 19 B.C., at the age of nearly fifty-one. He was buried outside Naples.

Even before undertaking his last journey Vergil had tried to extract from Varius the promise that, if anything happened to him, Varius should destroy the manuscript, but the latter did not agree. On his death-bed Vergil wanted the scrolls so that he himself could burn them but they were not given to him. His last wish, that Varius and Tucca should do so after his death, was opposed by Augustus in person. Although the work might not stand up to the severe self-criticism of its creator, it was too important to allow it to perish; Rome and the world had a right to it. Varius was entrusted with the publication. He proceeded with the greatest piety, removed but little and added nothing; he even let the incomplete half-lines stand.

When Vergil, twenty-eight years old, turned to pastoral poetry, he was no longer a novice. He himself mentions earlier poetic attempts, and Pollio's suggestion of writing bucolics shows that Vergil had already developed a distinct poetic individuality. According to an ancient *Vita*, his early works include the *Ballista, Catalepton, Dirae, Ciris, Culex, Aetna, Copa* and *Moretum*.

For the *Ballista* epigram we have only the authority of the 'Lives'; the remaining poems have been handed down to us as a collection. The *Culex* is an epyllion in the style of the New Poets. A shepherd, asleep in a grove, would have been killed by a poisonous snake, had he not been awakened in time by the bite of a gnat. The shepherd, however, before seeing the danger, strikes down the gnat. In the night his rescuer appears to him in a dream, complains of his ingratitude and describes in detail its experiences in the underworld. When he awakes the shepherd erects a gravestone to the gnat with a suitable inscription. The small, almost epigrammatic incident is expanded through insertions (praise of a shepherd's life, catalogue of the trees in the grove and of the flowers on the grave, the underworld) to a short epic, which plays adeptly on the contrast of high style and minor occasion. *Ciris* tells of the story of Scylla, who out of love for the enemy Minos deprived her father of the golden lock, the talisman of his life and of the safety of his city; but the victor Minos rejects the traitress and drags her, tied to his ship, through the sea. Scylla is turned into a sea-bird (*ciris*) whom her father chases as a sea-eagle. *Ciris* is a poem of considerable merit. The *Dirae* are a set of maledictions on the Alexandrian pattern, curses by a dispossessed landowner on the man to whom had fallen his Sicilian estate and the girl Lydia whom he had to leave behind there. Without interruption the manuscripts join to this a second poem, for which the title *Lydia* has become customary: the lament of an unlucky lover for the loss of his Lydia. It is a passionate poem, akin to elegy in its theme, if not in form and style. In *Copa* a Syrian landlady invites a wanderer to wine, women and dice. The *Moretum* describes realistically, parodying epic style, how a poor peasant prepares his rustic meal and then goes to his day's work. *Aetna* is a didactic poem on volcanism, scientific, and in conscious opposition to the mythical explanation of the phenomenon; the poet ends by describing an eruption of Etna, during which, to add a touch of human *pietas* and its miraculous reward, Amphion and his brother carry their parents on their shoulders safely through the lava.

Vergil's authorship for each of these poems has been questioned. That Vergil began as a New Poet is shown by the *Eclogues*. In his youth he admired Catullus, of whom his people at home were very proud, and Lucretius, whose work was perhaps made known to him in the circle of Siro. This makes the attribution of similar poems to him understandable. Whether Vergilian or not, they belong to the New Poetry. Some may be post-Vergilian: something of the New Poetry lived on alongside the Augustan classicism and even beyond. The question of authorship is still open; this much, however, may be asserted, that some pieces in the collection of small poems (*Catalepton*) are almost certainly by Vergil. At this stage he was still feeling his way. He was strongly, though not exclusively, influenced by Catullus; he had sufficient confidence in his talent to try his hand at the most different styles and subjects.

The *Eclogues* show Vergil for the first time as master of his art. The bucolic poetry is a creation of the Sicilian Greek Theocritus, who lived under Hiero II of Syracuse at the time of the first Punic war; later he went to Alexandria, where the new genre became at once popular. Theocritus called his poems '*eidyllia*', 'little sketches'; they have much in common with the mimes, except that the characters are almost always Sicilian shepherds and that the poet wrote in the Doric dialect of his native island. The poems of Theocritus and his followers were published in Rome in the time of Sulla, but they were little read, presumably on account of their unfamiliar dialect. Vergil's pastoral poetry was the first of its kind to influence European literature.

The title *Eclogues* ('Selections') which the ten poems bear in the manuscripts need not suggest that Vergil admitted only a selection of his bucolic poetry into the published collection. It refers to the individual poems as distinct artistic entities, each of which may be 'selected' at the reader's pleasure.

The poems are not arranged in the same order as they were written. Historical clues date *Ecl.* 1 and 9 as of the year 41 B.C., *Ecl.* 8 as of 39 B.C. The fourth falls in the year of Pollio's consulate, 40 B.C., probably in the autumn, after the peace of Brundisium, the tenth, on the testimony of the author himself, was the last to be written (*extremum laborem*). The poet so arranged his 'book' that pieces of a similar type would not follow immediately on one another.

When Vergil turned to pastoral poetry, he may have had nothing more in mind than to introduce the Theocritean genre to Roman literature. But even the earliest pieces, in which he still adhered rather closely to Theocritus, became in his hands something different. There is no trace of the slightly ironical realism of the Alexandrian poet; Vergil's shepherds are just human beings. That the countryside is often named as Sicily is scarcely more than an adopted Theocritean setting; Vergil also speaks of his home, of the Mincio, of Mantua and Cremona. His shepherds live in no particular countryside; the theme of the *Eclogues* is country-life as such. So Vergil finally, in the fourth and tenth *Eclogues*, creates a poetic Arcadia; it became part of the aesthetic heritage of Europe; in the end, inevitably, a cliché. The poet can now use the shepherd-song, no longer a naïve one, to speak in his own person of himself and his friends. The inspiration for this also came from Theocritus, who, in his 'Harvest feast', introduces himself and his friends as shepherds; but while this is merely a masquerade, Vergil sometimes lets his own person enter for a while into one of his characters, though without identifying himself with it entirely. Even *Ecl.* 1 and 9 are, despite the political background of the land assignments, not in a tangible sense autobiographical. The 'divine youth' (Octavian) does not, after all, reinstate the expelled shepherd in his property; the message implies quite generally that life on the 'good earth' is to go on undisturbed. That Vergil even then saw in the go-ahead power-politician the future saviour is more than the loyalty of a Transpadanian for Caesar and his heir: if not prophecy, it is at least intuition.

Imitation of Theocritus, never slavish, became more and more free in the later poems. Thus Vergil combines contrasting poems of Theocritus into a new unity, *e.g.* in *Ecl.* 8 the lament of the boy who is unlucky in love (Theocr. 1) and the successful love-charm of the girl (Theocr. 2: the happy ending belongs to Vergil). *Ecl.* 3 and 7 are singing contests of shepherds before an adjudicator (cf. Theocr. 5); in the one instance the contest remains undecided, in the other, one participant wins. The theme of *Ecl.* 6, dedicated to Varus as the simple homage of a bucolic poet, incompetent to write anything greater, is poetry itself. Silenus, asleep and drunk, is fettered by shepherds with his own garland; he willingly consents to free himself by singing. The contents of his song extend over the entire gamut of poetic subjects: there are all the favourite themes of the Alexandrians and their Roman pupils; only the beginning — the creation of the world and its primaeval stage — goes back to Hesiod. Gallus is the hero of *Ecl.* 10: in Arcadia Vergil, as a shepherd, sings a song of consolation for his friend, who has been deserted by the lady of his elegies, Lycoris. All nature sympathizes with Gallus's grief; the shepherd gods, Apollo and Pan, counsel moderation and reason. Gallus — at this point Vergil transposes elements of his friend's elegies into his own bucolic style — would love to be at home in this Arcadian world; and yet, he cannot escape the reality of his love, which is as boundless as is his pain; even though Lycoris is unfaithful, he feels for her only loving solicitude. After a confession of his friendship for Gallus, Vergil ends the poem by evoking the peaceful calm of a rural evening.

Ecl. 6 and 10, and in a different way 1 and 9, are interwoven with elements which are outside the bucolic world and blend with it only by the poet's skill in moving almost imperceptibly between several levels of reality. The fourth *Eclogue* finally transcends the pastoral; its actual subject lies outside the bucolic world, but bucolic themes are often echoed in details. An oracle of the Sibyl (*Cumaeum carmen*) has announced the return of the *Saturnia regna*; the cycle of the great world-year is ended; the iron age is about to be followed by a new golden one; not in a sudden change, but rather by a gradual transition, accompanying the growing up of a divine child who is to come to the world in this 'year of salvation', the consulate of Pollio. The boy will one day take his place among the gods and heroes; the fates give their blessing to the new order which is imminent. To live to see this is the poet's greatest desire; then he would even excel Pan, then his Arcadia would be reality. The ancients already sought in this poem a hidden meaning. In Vergil's lifetime Pollio's son Asinius Gallus claimed to be the boy of the *Eclogue*; the early church interpreted the poem as messianic.

With the *Georgics*, Vergil stepped out of his Arcadia into the Italy of his time. It is a poem about the work and life of the Roman peasant, as he had once seen himself, and as Octavian wanted to see him again: *vir bonus colendi peritus* ('a good man and a good farmer'). Vergil, familiar as he was from his childhood with life on the land and the work of the country-dweller, would, of course, also study literature on the subject; but however much of this may have gone into the *Georgics*, they are not didactic poetry in the technical sense. Vergil not only goes materially beyond the subject (*e.g.* with a study of the skies after the *Phaenomena* of Aratus), but transcends it. In the life of the peasant he contemplates the essence of human life in general;

peasant work is to him the root and also the symbol of culture. To be human, man must reach out into nature, selecting, arranging, and shaping its potentialities; but, being himself a part of nature, he is under her law; he cannot do as he pleases. In nature there is no lack of the hostile and fearsome: pests in the crops of field and tree, fire and tempest, epidemics. Nor does the earth give of its own accord. We live in an iron age, not under Saturn, but under Jupiter who wills man to toil; yet the compulsion to work spurs him to all those forms of inventiveness (*artes*) on which human culture is based. In nature man has an unequal and incalculable opponent; he therefore needs the blessing of the gods. The gods, however, only help him who helps himself. Nature is man's great teacher. While the bull shows his wild passion unsubdued, while the bees build a state whose perfection surpasses human comprehension, man must consciously realize the law which works in the cosmos as a natural force. From this, however, humanity has strayed farther and farther; a glimpse into the present reveals a terrifying chaos. Only where the timeless form of country-life survives has a little 'Arcadian' innocence remained; the *iustissima tellus* has preserved traces of that 'justice' which vanished from the earth with the end of the golden age. The only salvation is a return to the roots of human nature, which is most manifest in the life of the peasant. Octavian's victory has made this return possible, and he aims at bringing it about; may the gods, among whom the poet even now invokes him, allow his good work to come to fruition.

After this attempt to convey the message of the poem, we turn to the details. The poet's devotion to his task — Vergil worked on the *Georgics* from 36 to 29 B.C. — has achieved a perfection in verse-construction, language and composition scarcely to be surpassed: 'the best poem of the best poet' (Dryden).

The material is divided into four large subjects, each of which fills one book: agriculture, tree- and vine-growing, cattle-rearing and bee-keeping. But the large fundamental themes are all touched upon already in the first book and run through the whole work; the four books hang together like the movements of a symphony. Within the books the overall structure is clear, but not obtrusive. The famous 'digressions' (here hardly the right word) grow organically out of the context; not as added highlights, but as functional parts of the whole. Even a piece as topical as the celestial prodigies at Caesar's death is no exception: as the signs of weather and sky, about which the farmer must be knowledgeable, announce disturbances in nature, so omens fore-shadow dangers to the social order; both are laws of the same cosmos. The murder of Caesar has thrown the world into chaos; the plea to preserve the long-awaited saviour comes as a natural conclusion. The most famous of these 'digressions', the *laudes Italiae* (II, 136 ff.), becomes the focal point of the whole work. Here all the principal themes meet as it were polyphonic-ally.

At the end of this praise stands the line: *Ascraeumque cano Romana per oppida carmen* ('I sing a song of Ascra in the town-ships of Rome'). Ascra in Boeotia was the birthplace of Hesiod, whom later antiquity regarded as the inventor of the didactic poem, in modern terms: the first poet of ideas. Ideas, the fruit of reflection, were always presented by the ancients as a lesson. The poet of the *Georgics* wants to be a Roman Hesiod. He naturally had in mind Hesiod's 'Works and Days', which is related to the *Georgics* not only in its subject matter but also in its ethics. The succession of ages from gold to iron, hard work as a condition of well-being, the disappearance of justice, side by side with technical advice for farming and words of practical wisdom — all this Vergil found in his model. But the *Georgics*, inspired as they were by Hesiod, are essentially Vergilian in spirit. Even the starting-point is different. Hesiod's immediate concern is a private one. In a lawsuit against his brother Perses, corrupt judges had granted the family heritage to his idle brother; with his poem Hesiod wants to bring Perses on to the right road. Vergil's concern is a public one, not to call it official. At the same time it is his most personal concern. He also differs from Hesiod in his outlook. In place of the resignation of the disillusioned Greek, Vergil, without deceiving himself over hard reality, still has confidence: although he lives in the iron age, Italy, *magna parens frugum, magna virum* ('great mother of harvests and great mother of men') is potentially still Saturn's land.

Vergil is similarly indebted to his Roman model, Lucretius, whose style he perfects here as he does that of Ennius in the *Aeneid*. Lucretius looks on nature as an object, which he wants to explain; even in his most lively descriptions one feels a certain detachment. Vergil 'belongs', he takes part. In the famous passage, book 2, 480 ff., where he contrasts his poetry with that of Lucretius, he admits the greatness of his predecessor's world view; he himself is happy to belong to the world in which he lives: although not free from all fear, he feels at home there.

The fourth book strikes the reader as being in a special sense a labour of love. Never again was Vergil to come so completely under the spell of his subject. Like many poets before and after him, he was fascinated by the mysterious bees. According to a belief, common in antiquity, bees could be born of the blood of slaughtered cattle. This form of procreation was said to have been revealed to the shepherd Aristaeus, whose bees had died as a punishment for having caused the death of Eurydice. The epyllion of Orpheus and Eurydice, which forms the centre of Vergil's Aristaeus story, not only shows the poet at his best but is of the very substance of his message: for all the uncanny perfection of the *vie des abeilles*, man has, potentially, something greater — love, which is stronger even than death. If Vergil, as Servius tells us, had originally concluded this book with a praise of Gallus, and only after the latter's fall from grace, at the request of Augustus, substituted for it the Aristaeus legend, we have all the more reason for admiring the poet, who succeeded in welding the old and new elements into such a perfect whole that the uninformed reader would never guess what happened.

In the *Georgics*, this apotheosis of Roman peasant life, history is not more than an undercurrent, in the *Aeneid* it becomes the predominating dimension. Even before the *Eclogues* Vergil had at one time thought of the *res Romanae* as the subject of a poem but had abandoned the plan as uncongenial. In the *Georgics* he announced his intention of celebrating the deeds of Octavian. But if Vergil was seriously thinking of a panegyric he was too much of an artist not to reject the idea in the end. The achievement of Augustus had to be placed in a great mythological and historical context; only in this way could it be seen in its true significance, and become the subject of a great poem, immortalizing a historical moment. The idea of projecting Augustus into the Aeneas legend was suggested by the genealogy of the Julians, who claimed descent from the Trojan Aeneas and worshipped in his mother Venus the divine ancestress of their family. Caesar had actually consecrated a temple to Venus Genetrix in 46 B.C. The legend which connects Aeneas with the origins of Rome had been told by generations of annalists; Naevius (who also knew of Dido and her sister Anna) and Ennius had included it in their epics. Now Vergil set out to reveal in the story of Aeneas those seeds of Roman history which had come to full flowering under Augustus. No wonder that a poem so wide in scope and so full of meaning should enshrine the spiritual heritage of the world to which it was given: history and legend, religion and philosophy, the fullness of artistic possibilities which the poetry of the Greeks and Romans had discovered. To this day it has not ceased to be a living force in the poetry and thought of Europe.

For convenience we indicate here briefly the contents of the *Aeneid*. I: When Aeneas is already near his promised new home in the West, he is driven with his men on to the African coast by a storm raised at the instigation of Troy's enemy, Juno. They are received by Queen Dido in her newly founded Carthage. II–III: At a banquet in his honour Aeneas tells Dido of

the fall of Troy, of his divinely-ordained flight with his old
father Anchises, his son Ascanius and the Trojan Penates (II),
and of his eventful voyage through the Eastern Mediterranean
(III), which includes a landing at Actium, the new home of the
Trojan prophet Helenus, and the death of Aeneas's father in
Sicily. IV: Juno, who wants to frustrate hopes of a new Troy,
joins with Venus to bind Aeneas to Dido. The queen, filled
with passionate love for her guest, breaks her resolution to
remain faithful to her dead husband Sychaeus and tries to keep
Aeneas with her, against his destiny. Aeneas succumbs and so
completely forgets his mission that Jupiter has to remind him of
his task through Mercury. As Dido's desperate pleas to Aeneas
fail, she curses the involuntarily faithless man and kills herself.
V: On the journey to Italy a storm forces the sailors to land in
Sicily. It is the anniversary of the death of Anchises, and Aeneas
holds magnificent memorial games for his father. Meanwhile
Juno has persuaded the women in Aeneas's company to go no
farther; they set fire to the ships to prevent the continuation of
the voyage. On Aeneas's prayer, sudden rain quenches the fire,
but the lack of confidence of his people makes him nearly despair
of his mission. Anchises appears to him in a dream: Aeneas
must settle the half-hearted in Sicily, but continue with the
others to follow his goal; on his arrival in Italy he must first of
all visit his father in the underworld, so that the latter can unveil
to him the great future, destined for his new foundation. VI:
Landing at Cumae. Led by the Sibyl and protected by a golden
bough of magical powers, Aeneas enters the underworld at Lake
Avernus. He meets various people, among them Dido, and
eventually finds his father in Elysium. Anchises shows his son
the souls which will one day be reborn as great Romans: representatives of the Roman world, whose historical destiny is
announced in a celebrated passage (847 ff.). Aeneas reascends to
the earth. VII: On his landing in Latium, Aeneas sends a legation to King Latinus; the latter, obeying an ancient oracle,
receives the men honourably and offers Aeneas the hand of his

daughter Lavinia. But Juno stirs up a quarrel between Trojans and Latins which soon leads to war. Latinus himself stays out of it; the leader is the heroic, but overbearing, Rutulian Turnus, who demands Lavinia for himself and who is backed by Queen Amata. VIII: Aeneas seeks allies. Evander, who rules over the place where later Rome will be built, gives him troops under the leadership of his young son Pallas; another ally is won in the Etruscan Tarchon. On Venus's request Vulcan forges Aeneas's arms, among them a shield on which prophetic scenes from Roman history are represented. IX: In Aeneas's absence the Trojans are hard-pressed by Turnus. During the night Nisus and his friend Euryalus try to make their way through the enemy camp to carry news of the danger to Aeneas; but through the rashness of Euryalus both meet their death. On the next day the Trojans again fight an unsuccessful battle. Book X begins with an assembly of the gods, in which Jupiter reprimands both Juno and Venus for their intervention in the struggle; on this day the fortune of war has to run its course un-influenced. Aeneas enters into the fight. Turnus has just had an easy victory over the young Pallas, takes his armour from him and even mocks the dying man. Aeneas is bent on avenging Pallas, but Juno manages to rescue Turnus on this occasion. Aeneas finds an opponent in Mezentius; his son Lausus covers the retreat of his wounded father at the price of his own life. XI: During the truce for the burial of the dead, Aeneas proposes to decide the war by a duel between himself and Turnus; Latinus is prepared to come to an agreement, but Turnus presses for the continuation of the war. When, however, his ally, the heroic Camilla, is killed, his battle plan miscarries. Aeneas is marching up to the city. XII: The duel is to take place on the following day. But the Rutulians break their word and the fight begins anew. Not until Aeneas storms the town of Latinus, stripped of defenders, does Turnus come to meet him. Juno can no longer delay fate; but Jupiter grants that Latium shall not become a new Troy, that Aeneas and his fellows will become

Latins. Turnus is defeated and begs for mercy. Aeneas is inclined to spare him, but his eye catches sight of the spoils of Pallas, which Turnus bears, and he knows he has no right to grant him pardon. With the death blow which Turnus receives, the *Aeneid* comes to an end.

In the composition of the poem, a division into two parts (I–VI and VII–XII, 'Odyssey' and 'Iliad', journey to the new home and the fight for it) and one into three parts (I–IV: Aeneas in Carthage, V–VIII: journey to Latium and preparation for the fight, IX–XII: the decisive battles) overlap. Yet neither these groups nor the individual books are composed as strictly separate units. There are not only links between individual books but also themes and motifs which run through the whole work.

Vergil's sources and models are numerous and varied. Doubtless he not only knew several forms of the Aeneas legend differing from each other in details and freely made use of them; he was also familiar with the (strongly hellenized) traditions of ancient Italy (Oscan, Umbrian, Etruscan) and of Sicily. In his underworld, elements of the Homeric *Nekyia* are combined with religious and philosophical teachings (*e.g.* the stoic teaching of the world-soul, the Orphic idea of purification, the Pythagorean metempsychosis) as his artistic purpose would require; some details, such as the fairy-tale motif of the golden bough or the idea that the souls of the future Romans already have their earthly shapes, cannot be traced in earlier literature.

The chief poetic models are Homer and Ennius. Against all critics of his *furta*, ancient and modern, Vergil has justly remarked that it would be easier to snatch away Hercules's club than a single line from Homer. A heroic epic had to be 'Homeric'; that was demanded by the poetic tradition of antiquity. Vergil shows himself as a follower of Homer not only in elements of style (epithets, formulae, similes and recurring lines), not only in the adaptation (and remodelling) of themes, situations and episodes, but even in composition (*e.g.* in the story of Aeneas's voyage being told after his rescue from shipwreck). Yet it is always Homer with a difference. Vergil shifts the point of emphasis from the events to the experience of the hero, which he shares almost as if they were his own. The poet thus realizes the significance of that experience, and interprets history in the light of his own historical situation. On this basis each traditional element is given a new function.

Homer's heroes are typified individuals. Vergil's Aeneas is the idealized representative of his people; he lacks individuality. As the model Roman he is always *magnanimus* and *pius*. Although the Homeric hero cannot escape his destiny, he is at least master of his decisions; for Aeneas his divine destiny to become the ancestor of the Romans, is his sole *raison d'être*. The Homeric epics tell their story for its own sake; the fate of Aeneas always points back to Troy and forward to Rome. This fate, *fatum* (more frequently *fata*), however, is also the meaning of world history, as the Romans of Vergil's time would see it. The *fata* (this too is not Homeric) are identical with Jupiter, who thus stands as high above Juno, who does not accept them, as above Venus, who is over-anxious to ensure their fulfilment. On earth Dido, whose knowledge of Aeneas's *fata* is thrust aside by her passion, and Turnus, who vainly ignores them, bring about their own downfall. Aeneas follows the fates, at first not independently, but in obedience to his father, then gropingly and irresolutely, finally in free and conscious co-operation. Stage by stage his task, vaguely indicated in the beginning, becomes more clearly defined. In this sense Aeneas certainly undergoes a sort of development, but it is really a Pilgrim's Progress. Of course his way is also a way of suffering, as suffering is of the essence of this world: but where there is an aim there is hope.

Against this background the fate of each individual (Dido, Nisus and Euryalus, Evander and Pallas, Mezentius and Lausus, Camilla) takes on a romantic character. Considered by themselves, these episodes are among Vergil's finest work. Nobody puts before us the death of young people (Euryalus, Pallas, Camilla) more movingly, and yet without sentimentality. At the same time, these episodes have a definite function within the work. All these episodic figures are surpassed in importance by Dido. That Aeneas must leave her is not only (as in Naevius) the cause of the enmity between Rome and Carthage. Her presence is felt throughout the poem: when she meets Aeneas in the underworld, she turns away from him without a word; yet her memory haunts him — and us — as a shadow. She is as it were the building-sacrifice of the empire-builder.

The battle scenes are somewhat lifeless. Vergil is on the height of his suggestive power where he evokes the solemn and the numinous, *e.g.* in the numerous prodigies. Numinous as a whole is Aeneas's visit to the Arcadian Evander, on the site of the future Rome: here, characteristically, 'Arcadian' motifs reappear.

The Ennian element in the *Aeneid* is less problematic. A subdued echo of Ennian verse and formulae was intended to give an impression of archaic dignity without archaic heaviness; in the new Roman epic the old was to echo again and again.

Does the *Aeneid* show traces of its unfinished condition? Certainly in the half-lines. From the point of view of composition, books III and X give the impression of being left unrevised, especially for a certain lack of consistency in the chronological correlation of events. The fact that (apart from the half-lines) penetrating analysis is necessary to discover such traces shows the high standards of the Augustan poet. Of course, small discrepancies in details remain. They are found in any writing of large extent. Vergil might have invoked the precedent of the *Iliad* and *Odyssey*.

The greatness of Vergil's work was realized already by his contemporaries. Q. Caecilius Epirota, a freedman of Atticus, introduced the study of Vergil into school, where it has still its place. Equally strong was Vergil's influence on later poetry and

5. Vergil and two of the Muses: a mosaic from Hadrumetum

6. From the Ara Pacis, Rome: Tellus (Mother Earth) with Air and Water

7. Priests and part of the Imperial family from the Ara Pacis: Agrippa, Iulia, Tiberius and Lucius Caesar

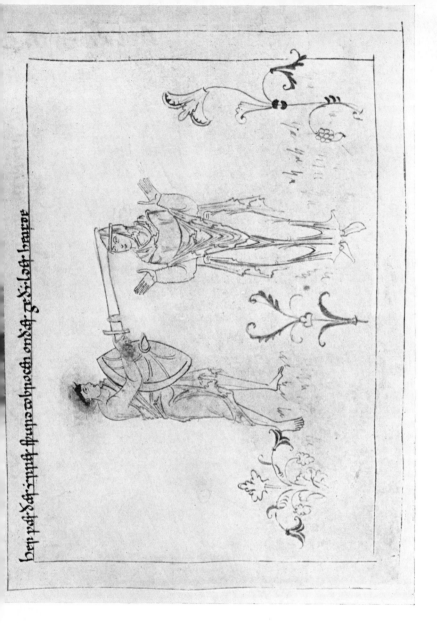

8. An illustration
to the *Psychomachia*
of Prudentius:
Ira vainly trying
to kill Patientia

even on elevated prose. In late antiquity he was held in as high esteem among educated Christians as among the Roman 'nationalists'. Even the young Augustine was under his spell.

The middle ages saw in Vergil not only a model of Latin style, but a forerunner of Christianity; from the twelfth century Vergil even counted as a magician. Imitation of Vergil runs through the whole of mediaeval poetry. There were epics in the Vergilian tradition: the Waltharius poem, the Alexander poem of Walter of Châtillon, and the Trojan War of Joseph of Exeter. Even the vernacular epic, *e.g.* the Song of Roland or the Nibelungenlied, is indebted to Vergil. Dante's relationship to Vergil is different: no longer adaptation, but rebirth; this is also essentially true of the great epics of the early modern period. The rediscovery of Homer temporarily eclipsed Vergil's fame, especially in Germany, but brought forth no great poetry of Homeric inspiration. The reason may be found partly in the literary situation of the time.

If there was nothing magic about Vergil's person, his art might truly be so described. No other poet has realized all the possibilities of the hexameter with such artistic economy, or has conveyed so suggestively the symbolism of his story in equally simple and transparent language, or has been able to maintain such a perfect balance between the elaboration of details and the unity of the whole.

Q. HORATIUS FLACCUS

There are hardly two more contrasting human types than those of Vergil and the Southerner Horace. We can picture him vividly to ourselves: small and nimble; rather stout in middle age (Augustus teased him about it in a letter); not averse to the joys of wine and love, without losing himself in them; a keen observer, inclined to scepticism, critical and self-critical, careful to preserve his independence in thought and life and just for that reason an upright and reliable friend; 'a pig from the herd of Epicurus', as he calls himself, but a Roman epicurean who finds pleasure in a life according to nature, in an enlightened concept of *virtus*, free from stoic dogmatism and rigour; gifted with a sense for the real thing, a taste for simplicity, and an infallible tact in all walks of life. Being such a man, he was able to appreciate the achievement of Augustus and the intentions behind his reforms, and became, after Vergil, the most important witness to the spirit of the Augustan era, and one of the creators of its image in poetry.

Horace was born on 8th December 65 B.C. in Venusia, on the border of Lucania and Apulia. His father was a freedman, who throughout his life never changed his lower-class manners. But for the talented Quintus he did everything in his power: instead of sending him to the school of the provincial town where the sons of centurions, offspring of the veterans of Sulla, set a low tone, the father, though a man of limited means, went to Rome with his son and took him to the school of the renowned grammarian Orbilius. There the *Odyssey* of Livius Andronicus was first beaten into him; later he read the *Odyssey* in the original. From Rome, Quintus went to Athens to pursue philosophical studies. Like so many of his fellow-students, in autumn 44 B.C. he joined the army of Brutus. He survived the battle of Philippi, in which he had taken part as a military tribune; but the career which a victory of Brutus would have opened for him had come to nothing. His father's house and estate had been confiscated by the Triumviri, and Horace had to see about earning his living. He bought a post as *scriba quaes-torius* (secretary of the state treasury and archives), which assured him a livelihood, but cannot have given him much satisfaction. In his off-hours he wrote poetry. Horace had certainly written verse as a student, as was fashionable; but now he took poetry seriously. Success soon came his way. Vergil and Varius recommended the young poet to Maecenas. The first intro-duction to the influential man was a painful experience: Horace only stammered a little about his humble birth; after a short while, Maecenas dismissed him with some non-committal words.

For nine months Maecenas made no move ; then he accepted
Horace into his circle.   The journey to Brundisium which he
undertook as a companion of Maecenas (37 B.C.) shows Horace
already at home in his new environment ; soon he was the
possessor of a country estate in the Sabine hills, a present which
delighted him throughout his life.

The first book of satires (*Sermones*) would seem to have been
completed in 35 B.C., the second book and the *Iambi* (epodes) in
30 B.C. In both works we see the spirited young poet progress-
ing not only from the imitation of literary forms to sovereign
mastery but also from political defeatism to a personal concern
about the new order that was beginning to take shape.

The *Iambi* have their origin in the social life of early Greece.
In that world they were the normal form of personal or political
invective.   The master of this form was Archilochus of Paros
(seventh century B.C.) ; it is in his style and spirit that Horace
tried to write.   He took over from the Greeks the Iambic
trimeter.   What he could not take over was the unrestrained
attack on people in public life.   The few individuals whom he
personally attacked — the poetaster Mevius, the sorceress
Canidia, the usurer Alfius — are people without importance.

In the *Sermones* Horace challenges Lucilius, whose manly
spirit and satirical bite he admired as much as he disliked his
careless style, his unconcern about purity of language, and his
cumbersome versification.   Horace wants to re-create Lucilian
satire for his own time as Vergil re-created the Ennian epic ; so
we see him take up many of Lucilius's themes.   Here, however,
Horace had to face the same difficulty as in his iambic poetry.
Lucilius's uncompromising criticism of his contemporaries was
no longer possible, least of all for one of the humble origin and
political past of Horace.   Again the people whom he attacks
are, politically, nobodies.   In some instances the attack is only a
starting-point.   Thematically the criticism of society (*e.g.* for
adultery, legacy-hunting and snobbish entertainment) is less in

evidence than the 'philosophy of the market-place' after the manner of Bion of Borysthenes (third century B.C.). A 'Bionian' theme is, *e.g.*, the dissatisfaction with one's own life and the envy of somebody else's, or the 'pep-talk' of the slave Davos, who, availing himself of the Saturnalian freedom of speech, holds up a mirror to his master, Horace. Such *Sermones* often take on the form of fictitious dialogue. Horace is at his best where he talks about the little happenings of everyday life (*e.g.* how he tried to shake off an importunate passer-by on the road), where he speaks of his relationship with Maecenas, or contrasts a busy day in the city with the idyll of his Sabine estate. Horace developes the diverse ingredients, the fable with its obvious moral, diatribe, dialogue, *exempla*, to the highest degree and makes his language, style and differentiating treatment of the hexameter the perfect instrument of his artistic intentions. The normal level of polite conversation is raised or lowered according to subject and mood, from the language of prayer to gross realism or to epic parody.

When Horace in 23 B.C. published three books of *carmina* (called 'odes' by later commentators), he realized that he had conquered new territory for Roman literature. His claim to be the first 'to have sung the Aeolian song in the Italian manner' was valid even after the Sapphic poems of Catullus and his prayer to Diana. Only Horace, the most Greek and at the same time the most Roman of Rome's poets, could dare to imitate the ancient Greek lyric, the highest and most inaccessible form of Greek poetry, whose masters (Pindar, Bacchylides, Anacreon, Alcaeus and Sappho) were now only great names even in their own country.

Horace probably experimented with lyric poetry already at the time of his last epodes, some of which scarcely differ from the odes in theme and style. His 'Ship of State' (I, 14) is more likely to have been written before than after Actium. Even such a masterpiece as *Nunc est bibendum* (I, 37) was surely written soon after the death of Cleopatra (30 B.C.).

In referring to his lyric as *Aeolium carmen*, Horace was obviously thinking in the first place of the metrical form. His odes represent Greek lyric poetry almost in its entire range; but he has neither constructed 'Anacreontea' nor imitated the elaborate stanzas of the choral lyric. His metres are Aeolian; for more than half the poems he employs the Alcaic or Sapphic stanza. He also gathers together pairs of epodes (*i.e.* of a longer line followed by a shorter one), or such lines as Asclepiads, into stanzas of four lines. Contrary to the free handling of these metres by the Greeks, where only the number of syllables is constant, Horace adheres to one pattern for each type of verse. The strict observance of caesura is also new. Horace follows not a metrical theory but traditional practice and his own musical feeling.

Horace took over themes from Alcaeus more often than from other poets, *e.g.* the Ship of State (I, 14) or the complaint of Neobule (III, 12). He likes to echo some lines of Alcaeus as a motto in the beginning of a poem and in this way to set it against a famous Greek one. But many odes, so far as we can see, have no Greek model; they are free creations in an adopted style. From Sappho, Horace has only the stanza form; he was enough of a poet to feel that she was inimitable. He hesitated for a long time to rival Pindar: odes I, 12 and III, 4 belong to the later poems of the collection. Not until the fourth book, which followed the first three after a number of years, did Horace succeed in transposing him into his own, now fully developed, lyric style.

The Lesbian song was sung to the lyre; but in the odes of Horace this is a stylistic convention. Horace wrote for recitation and reading; only the *Carmen saeculare* was intended to be performed by a choir of boys and girls.

Not every piece in the collection is perfect; as in his early books of poetry, here too Horace deliberately retained some 'studies', *e.g. Vides ut alta* (I, 9: 'pretty verses, but still no poem', says Wilamowitz) or the Paris ode (I, 15). Of course

the arrangement of the poems is not chronological; the govern-
ing principle is that of thematic and metrical variation. Only
the group of patriotic Roman odes (III, 1–6) forms, in both
aspects, a unit. At the beginning of book I (I, 2–9) Horace displays his characteristic verse-forms one after the other. These
poems are dedicated to important persons: Augustus, Vergil,
Sestius (consul of the year of publication), Agrippa, etc. The
collection is framed by poems to Maecenas (I, 1 and III, 30).

Horace saw in the odes the culmination of his poetic art;
these were to make him immortal. The modern reader, on
the other hand, finds the way to Horace's lyric most difficult.
One must not approach it with the romantic idea of poetry.
But even measured against the lyric of the Lesbians, Horace is
to a high degree stylized. In the well-known dialogue poem
III, 9 (*Donec gratus eram tibi*) the lovers are divested of all individuality. Every theme is reduced to its basic form, and the sus-
tained parallelism is reminiscent of a rococo dance; but in its
deliberate artificiality, the poem still has intense life. Even
where Horace speaks of himself, he likes to hide behind typical
situations and reflections; but he often gives traditional themes
a personal touch. He shows most of his own self in poems of
friendship, *e.g.* in the prayer for a safe journey for Vergil (I, 3)
or in some of the Maecenas odes (I, 20; II, 17).

What the gods, about whom we hear so much, meant to
Horace is not easy to say. To introduce a vision of Bacchus (II,
19) with *credite posteri* is no profession of faith; but the sacrifice
to the fountain of Bandusia (III, 13), which only the poem has
made immortal, is a genuine sacred act, and his thanksgiving
to the Muse (IV, 3) is more than a mere metaphor. The sceptical
Horace never lost his sense for the *numen*; to the poet the gods
were not mere aesthetic fiction, and their worship was more than
mere form. Proof of this is the *Carmen saeculare*, and its prelude,
the Roman odes. The poet, *Musarum sacerdos*, now speaks as a
teacher and adviser; having learned from experience the value
of a simple and truly human life, he sees in the return to such a

life — the idea of the *pax Augusta* — salvation for Rome. Together with the warning of Juno (III, 3) and the example of Regulus (III, 5), his own chosen way of life (III, 1, 47 f.) can be an inspiration for others.

The success of the odes with the Roman public fell rather short of the poet's expectations. Disappointed, Horace turned away from great poetry and took up once more the philosophizing *sermones*, which to him were not real poetry at all. So between 23 and 20 B.C. the first book of *Epistles* came to be written.

The opening poem, addressed to Maecenas, takes its cue from Horace's decision to abandon great poetry. The twenty letters all have addresses, and so appear as messages to individual persons; yet from the beginning they were written with a public in mind. The bite of the satires has disappeared; mature wisdom is presented with perfect *urbanitas*. The old theme of 'town and country' is resumed in the letter to his friend Aristius Fuscus (10) and in the (fictitious) answer to his steward, who is bored with country-life (13). Horace found life in Rome less congenial and more and more irksome with the years. Approaching old age also figures in the introductory and closing poems; in the latter the poet addresses his book, as if it were a handsome boy, to whom he predicts his inevitable decay to senility. More personal is the short letter to Tibullus (4) and the long one to Maecenas (7). Horace felt that Maecenas wanted to tie him too much to his person; he explains to the great man in all frankness that he would sooner give up anything than his independence; only in full personal freedom can he be his friend. Maecenas understood the poet and did not bear him a grudge; in his will he asked Augustus: *Horati Flacci ut mei esto memor* ('Look after Horace as if it were I').

With the second book of *Epistles* and the letter to the Pisones (*Ars poetica*) Horace turns to reflections on the nature of poetry. In the letter to *Florus* (*Epist.* II, 2) Horace once more explains in detail his reasons for giving up writing odes; there also he already professes those aesthetic principles which underlie the letter to the Pisones, where Horace formulates his renunciation most precisely. The address of the Pisones is merely a dedication; Horace is talking to all those who want to write poetry: he wants to guide those striving for perfection, and to frighten off the hopeless dilettantes. He gives an introduction to the art of poetry, using as a source the *Poetics* of Neoptolemos of Parium (third century B.C.). But Horace has much of his own to say. Speaking from his personal experience as a poet, he insists on the unremitting study of the *exemplaria Graeca* (not for slavish imitation, but in order to develop taste and judgement), on attention to artistic unity, on the correct handling of language, themes and character-drawing. In this spirit Petronius later praises in Horace the *curiosa felicitas*, the apparent facility of his perfection, which in reality is the reward of intensive effort. What Horace demanded above all from others and from himself, is the restraint, the artistic economy, his specifically 'Attic' classicism. It is characteristic that he shuns the exaggerating superlative. From his point of view Horace also criticized the earlier Roman literature, which still had its admirers, and especially the drama. That was the only form of poetry in which classical perfection was not achieved: neither the *Thyestes* of L. Varius Rufus, produced and royally honoured at the triumph of Octavian, and compared by Quintilian to the best tragedies of the Greeks, nor the *Trabeata* of Melissus was able to prevent the literary drama in Rome from dying out.

If the public failed to understand Horace, he found one reader to whom his art strongly appealed: Augustus. At the express desire of the *princeps*, Horace sent him a copy of his odes. Augustus even wanted to make Horace his private secretary, but Horace declined this appointment, honourable though it was. As a poet, he was stimulated to new work by the commission to write a song for the Secular Feast of 17 B.C., a processional hymn for a double choir of Roman boys and girls from the most distinguished families. As the Secular Feast itself, though reviving an early tradition, was none the less specifically a thanksgiving to the gods for the *pax Augusta* and a plea for its preservation, so the *Carmen saeculare*, though in the tradition of Roman ritual poetry, is characteristically Horatian and Augustan. It is composed in the Sapphic stanza, which Horace had learnt to master so perfectly. Here Horace identifies himself with the ideals of Augustus even more completely than in the Roman odes. The *Carmen saeculare* is the poetic counterpart to the *Ara Pacis*.

Thus encouraged, Horace turned again to lyric. Book IV of the odes (17–13 B.C.) shows him matured, but also aged and resigned. He looks back with pride and gratitude on his life's work, which the greatest man of his time had not found wanting. Horace, now a sort of poet laureate, celebrates great events like the victories of the emperor's stepsons Drusus and Tiberius (15–14 B.C.) in odes which capture as much of Pindar's spirit as Horace's style would allow; at the same time he tells Augustus in words of moving simplicity of Italy's longing for his return from Spain and Gaul. But for the poet himself the best years were past. The poet's dream of the boy Ligurinus, who continually escapes him (I, 37 ff.), stands symbolically at the beginning of the book; his invitation to the young Phyllis (11) is made on the assumption that her lover is untrue to her; his malicious joy over the aging of Lyce, who once rejected him (13) is tempered with melancholy memories of his love for young Cinara, who died before her beauty faded (hers is the only woman's name in the odes behind which there might be a real person). The spring song *Diffugere nives* (7), whose beginning is intended to remind the reader of *Solvitur acris hiems* (*Carm.* I, 4), is the work of a man who feels the winter coming and who knows that human life has no part in the enduring cycle of nature.

In the time of the last odes falls also the literary epistle to Augustus (*Epist.* II, 1). The *princeps* had personally asked

Horace to dedicate to him a letter in the style of the Florus and Piso letters. Horace takes this opportunity for a discussion of the role of poetry in Rome's past and present, and, in this light, reviews his own endeavours. Where his art is concerned, Horace can speak to the emperor with the informality of an equal and the frankness of a friend. Both are agreed on the place of poetry in the new Rome, but Horace has the gift of putting their views into words with an aptness that is deceptively casual.

Horace had already suffered many personal losses: Vergil and Tibullus had died in 19 B.C., Varius followed them in 14 B.C.; in 8 B.C. Maecenas died. Horace outlived him by only a few months; he died on 27th November of the same year and was buried near him on the Esquiline.

Horace's impact cannot be compared with that of Vergil. He, too, was soon studied in the schools, but he was never so widely read. His imitation in Christian antiquity and the middle ages was purely formal. Though much quoted (his *curiosa felicitas* gave him countless phrases of original pithiness) and an ancestor of literary criticism through his *Ars poetica*, he has never been popular. To an age like our own, Horace's *aurea mediocritas* might easily seem shallow. But the smoothness of form, the muted tone, the tendency towards understatement, the informal gesture can be deceptive. Horace is often more serious than he wants to appear, and more personal than he pretends to be. His generation knew chaos; it was all the more thankful to the man who had banished it. Banished, not conquered; Horace was not blind to that: his Roman odes end with a gloomy vision, and history has borne him out. An attempt to work against the destructive forces was none the less worth making; Horace, who began as a republican and always remained loyal to the memory of Cato, came to be a convinced supporter of Augustus. His odes reflect, as in a mirror, the peace Augustus had brought. They are a *monumentum aere perennius*, more lasting than even the poet could foresee.

TITUS LIVIUS

Livy shows himself much less affected by the specifically Augustan spirit than Horace or Vergil; but his historical work, whose perspective and artistic form have their roots in the world of Cicero, nevertheless belongs essentially to Augustan literature. Not only is Augustus for Livy a new Romulus: not only does he see, in the return to the old Roman spirit, salvation from moral decay: not only does he, like Vergil, revel in evoking the archaic aura of religious and state ceremonies: his work is as a whole a monument to *Romanitas* as revealed in Rome's history. Even if Livy could not say of his work *in medio mihi Caesar erit*, his image of the old Rome in contrast to the Rome of the last hundred years is essentially the same as that in the *Aeneid* or the 'Roman Odes' of Horace. It has as little to do with pragmatic history as with propagandist falsification. Livy builds a 'hall of honour' in words — a literary pendant to the marbles on the *forum Augusti*. Augustus recognized the importance of Livy's endeavour right from the beginning.

Born in Padua in 59 (or 64?) B.C., educated in rhetoric and interested in philosophy (he wrote a philosophico-historical dialogue and philosophical works in the narrower sense), Livy went to Rome in or before 30 B.C., and there dedicated himself in quiet seclusion to his life's work, a history of Rome from its origins (hence the title: *Ab urbe condita libri*) to the death of Drusus (9 B.C.). Still unknown as an author, he called attention to his work by readings of its early portions. His history seems to have been published in groups of five books, the first of which must have fallen between the conferring of the title of Augustus on Octavian (27 B.C.) and the second closure of the temple of Janus (25 B.C.). The 'Roman history' made its writer famous in his own lifetime; a man from Gades (Cadiz) travelled to Rome just to see Livy. In A.D. 17, Livy died at the age of seventy-five.

Of the one hundred and forty-two books *Ab urbe condita* only

1–10 and 21–45 remain. We possess information on the contents of the whole work; a shortened edition (*epitome*), which
goes back to the second century, was used by many later
historians.

Book 1 tells of the Roman kings; 2–5 cover the history or
the republic up to the Gallic invasion; 6–10 extend to the third
war with the Samnites (293 B.C.); 21–30 comprise the war with
Hannibal, 31–45 the events up to the triumph of L. Aemilius
Paulus (167 B.C.).

Livy neither studied primary sources nor travelled to the
scenes of the events which he related. The vastness of his subject
would scarcely have made that possible. His principal sources
are Claudius Quadrigarius and Valerius Antias, Coelius Antipater and Polybius; the last mentioned was his chief source for
Roman policy in the Greek East. The elder Cato might have
been directly used; the later books probably owe much to
Posidonius; and of course Livy also drew on the historical
writers of the post-Sullan era up to Asinius Pollio. Livy's
method is open to objections: he usually limited himself to
one source which he often supplemented and corrected from a
second. This process has resulted in a number of chronological
errors and even an occasional duplication of one and the same
event; we also encounter some misunderstandings in political
and military matters. Roman patriotism and partiality (*e.g.* for
the elder Scipio) have often led to a shift of emphasis or the
suppression of embarrassing detail, but never to a tangible
falsification of history.

In the spirit of later stoicism (Posidonius) Livy conceives of
history as a meaningful process. To him the ascent of Rome is
a work of Providence. The gods of the state religion he naturally accepted as symbolic, but he was convinced of a divine
world order, for which those gods stood. This world order
includes the moral law. He sees *pietas* and *virtus* as powers
that brought about the ascent of Rome, and blames their decline
for Rome's downfall. In details one may see a tendency

towards a more rationalistic interpretation of history, in particular where Livy has come under the influence of Polybius. He also tends to interpret history psychologically: the powers which are shaping history are at work in the minds and souls of its actors. Characteristic of Livy is his endeavour to penetrate to the minds of persons behind their actions; still more remarkable is his feeling for the plight of the distressed, the besieged and the conquered.

Following in the footsteps of Isocrates, whose theory governed hellenistic historical writing, Livy wanted to create a work of art, akin to poetry in style and treatment. Even though he subordinated the tendencies of the tragic-pathetic historiography of hellenism to historical truth, he still gives much room to episodes of emotional impact, to indirect characterization through a person's own words, and to impressive crowd scenes. While in the narrative parts the technique of Caesar is unmistakable, the formal speeches are in the tradition of Ciceronian rhetoric.

In many aspects Livy's language is late republican rather than Augustan; the transition to 'Silver Latin' is perceptible only in his syntax. In contrast to Sallust he uses archaisms only where he wants to create an archaic atmosphere, e.g. in the words of solemn prayers or formulae. Dactylic rhythms, which sometimes amount to hexameters, may be intentional as a poetic element; so, evidently, are echoes of Ennius. It is not always possible, however, to distinguish with certainty between the style of Livy and that of his Roman sources, which are in the same tradition.

To understand Livy as an artist is also to do him justice as a historian. The broad lines of his presentation have stood the test of time; even for the early period they have been corroborated by archaeology. In points of detail the value of his evidence varies with his source. Livy's historical perspective is not ours; but the way a Roman at the height of his civilization thought about his own past is in itself a historical fact of some importance.

Annals were also written by Livy's contemporary Fenestella (52 B.C.–A.D. 19). The Romanized Celt POMPEIUS TROGUS, a son of that Cn. Pompeius who in 54 B.C. was Caesar's interpreter, wrote in his forty-four books of *Historiae Philippicae* a universal history of the ancient world, with his focus on the ascent to power of Macedonia and its decay into the Diadochan kingdoms; Rome and the West were treated only in a supplement.

THE ELEGY

The elegy of the Augustans centres in the sphere of private life (*otium*) with its individual experiences. With the elegy of the Greeks, which we know from the seventh century B.C. onwards, it has little more in common than the metrical form, the elegiac couplet.

The Greeks described as *elegeia* every poem in the elegiac verse, which consists of a hexameter and pentameter. Short forms of elegiacs are the scolion and the epigram; we also know elegies of considerable length, like the political manifestos of Solon of Athens. The themes of elegy are most diversified: politics (Solon, Theognis), calls to battle (Callinus, Tyrtaeus), and worldly wisdom, of which a pessimistic hedonism is characteristic (Mimnermos). From the sixth century onwards the elegy also became a form of narrative lyric. The late epic poet Antimachus (about 400 B.C.) was the model for the elegiac love story of the Alexandrians.

The Romans took many themes over from the Greeks: the contrast of death and love, of the sorrows and joys of life, and also the heroic love story as a reflection of personal experience. Yet the Roman elegy cannot simply be traced back to the Greeks: its central theme is more subjective, and nothing really comparable exists in the surviving Greek elegies.

Although Catullus had anticipated the love elegy, credit for its 'invention' was given to CORNELIUS GALLUS; he was the first to publish a *book* of elegies and in so doing turned the

isolated instance of Catullus into a literary form. Born in 69
B.C., he attached himself early to Octavian and took part on
his side in the war against Antony. In 30 B.C. Octavian made
him *praefectus* of Egypt; soon, however, he fell into disfavour
through arrogance and indiscretion, and in 26 B.C. he committed suicide. As well as epyllions in the style of Euphorion,
Gallus wrote four books of elegies on his beloved Lycoris; but
only a single pentameter survives in quotation.

Indirectly we get an idea of the elegies of Gallus from the
speech which Vergil (*Ecl.* 10, 31 ff.) puts into his mouth. Lines
46–49 most probably reproduce lines of Gallus; the whole
speech is un-Vergilian in its themes and progress of ideas, and
resembles the poetry of Tibullus, Propertius and Ovid. Gallus
probably called his books of elegies *Amores*.

The Roman knight ALBIUS TIBULLUS wrote under the
influence of Catullus, but above all of Gallus. Of his life we
know but little. Tibullus seems to have suffered some loss of
property through the land allotments, but later he was in
possession of a farm near Pedum, and his *paupertas* must be
understood in the terms of his time and class. He served under
Messalla in the Aquitanian campaign (28–27 B.C.) and also
accompanied him on a mission to Asia, but illness forced him
to stay behind in Corcyra (1, 3). However, he felt happy only
in private life; like Vergil he loved to retreat to the country. His
poetry is the finest that was written in the circle around Messalla.
Tibullus died in 19 B.C. Ovid, who had got to know him in the
entourage of Messalla, dedicated an elegy to his memory.

Of the three books of elegies which go under Tibullus's name,
only the first two have come entirely from the poet's hand. In
the third book, *Elegies* 19 and 20 are certainly authentic: early
work, echoing the style of Catullus. Book III, 1–6, are elegies
of one Lygdamus (a pseudonym?) to his *coniunx* (wife or
mistress) Neaera. The author, who despite his technical skill
can hardly be called a poet, indicates his year of birth with the

same words as Ovid (*b.* 43 B.C.) does his: *cum cecidit fato consul uterque pari* (Tib. III, 5, 18 = Ovid, *Tristia,* iv, 10, 6). A panegyric on Messalla (III, 7), of uncertain date, is of no poetic value: the flattering letter of a sponging client. There follow two cycles (III, 8–12, and 13–18) on the same theme: the love of Messalla's niece Sulpicia for one Cerinthus. The poems of the second group are undoubtedly by Sulpicia herself; in their directness, uninhibited by artistic discipline, they are quite unique in Roman literature. The first cycle is the work of a poet of merit, in whom many would recognize Tibullus.

Tibullus's two books of elegies soon came to be known by the names of their heroines, 'Delia' and 'Nemesis'. Tibullus's Delia was presumably a lady of society; yet in the poems, in which she appears now as a married woman, now as a courtesan, she does not really come to life. Even less so does the Nemesis of book II. His love for Nemesis is represented as a reaction to Delia's infidelity. Delia does not wholly dominate book I, nor Nemesis book II: book I not only contains three poems on a boy Marathus, but also the lovely birthday poem for Messalla (7); in 1 and 3 Delia is not the central figure, in 10 she is as little named as Nemesis is in II, 1 and 2.

For the elegiac poet, privacy and leisure (*otium*) is the real substance of life. Other poets had deplored war and the restless striving after gain, but here this attitude is fundamental: devotion to a woman takes the place of devotion to the state, the *militia* of the lover contrasts with that of the soldier. Yet it is not the erotic poems with their conventional themes which show Tibullus's art at its purest, but those in which he sings of the simple life in rural seclusion, painted with the bucolic colours of the golden age, against the background of an afflicted and restless world (I, 1 and 10), or captures the relaxed mood of the Ambarvalian festival (II, 1) or of the celebration of his birthday (II, 2). But (unlike Vergil and Horace) Tibullus is not concerned with the *pax Augusta*: the name of Augustus is never mentioned. This hardly means opposition to the regime, but merely complete

submersion in his own world. His self-centredness is most evident in I, 3 : Tibullus, having stayed behind ill at Corcyra, lets
his thoughts slip in a melancholy manner back to his separation
from Delia and forward to presentiments of his death; instead
of the golden age he conjures up a vision of an Elysium for
lovers. The poem is also most characteristic of Tibullus because
of its tender mood and the flowing, often purely associative,
transitions in the sequence of mental images, thoughts and
emotions.

When Tibullus published his 'Delia', SEX. PROPERTIUS
presumably had already made a name for himself with his
Cynthia. He too takes after Gallus.

Propertius was an Umbrian, born in Asisium (Assisi). As a
child he lost his father in the Perusine war; most of the family
property was confiscated. However, Propertius was able to
study at Rome. Scarcely had he reached manhood when, un-
interested in a public career, he plunged into the social life of
the capital. He might have been nineteen years old when he
became embroiled with the courtesan Hostia; the relationship
with this cultured and refined, passionate and hot-tempered
woman, full of tormenting tension with rare moments of the
utmost happiness, lasted for at least five years. About 23 B.C.,
it would seem, the affair came to an end. Up to this time the love
for Hostia ('Cynthia' after the mountain Cynthos on Delos, the
birthplace of Artemis and Apollo) is the dominating theme of
Propertius's poetry.

The first book of elegies, published 29 or 28 B.C., bears, rightly,
Cynthia's name; she dominates it more than does Delia or
Nemesis in the elegies of Tibullus. Unfulfilled desires, a visit to
the sleeping mistress, jealousy (e.g. when Cynthia wants to go to
the fashionable Baiae), warning against a rival — these are some
of Propertius's themes. His language is intensely personal, his
style has a certain toughness and an archaic tinge. Passion is
mirrored in myth, as becomes a 'learned' poet. Behind his

F

rhetoric we feel genuine pathos. Propertius differs as much from Tibullus, who cares little about 'objectivating' his feelings, as from Ovid, whose main interest is in the concrete situation. The sequence of the poems does not recognizably reflect the successive phases of the erotic relation. Besides, each individual poem is a work of art in its own right; personal experience seems often to have served merely as a starting-point. The book also contains some poems to various friends of the poet, especially to Tullus (nephew of L. Volcacius Tullus, cos. 33 B.C.), to whom it is dedicated. The Cynthia book was an immediate success; even in the time of Martial it was still popular as a present.

The poet sought access to the circle of Maecenas. He worshipped Vergil; Horace kept apart, and seems to have criticized, at least indirectly, the style of Propertius, which he did not find to his taste.

Even if Propertius chose *otium* for himself, he reacted much more strongly to his environment than did Tibullus. The Cynthia book has room for the sufferings of the Perusine war (21 and 22). When Maecenas, to whom the second book of elegies is dedicated, asked him to write a glorification of Augustus, he replied with the customary apologies (1), but held out the prospect of such a poem when his powers would have increased (10). The book nevertheless contains a poem in which a contemporary event is bound up (superficially) with the love theme (31): Propertius has kept his mistress waiting because on his way to her he has been admiring the newly completed temple of the Palatine Apollo, which he then describes. This in itself is certainly a traditional theme; but Tibullus would never have been even as topical as that. Cynthia plays an essential role in this and also in the following book. He records the climax of their love relation, but also complains more and more about the faithlessness of his mistress and tells of his attempts to tear himself away from her power, leading up to bitter renunciation. In the third book new themes become prominent: reflexions on his own poetry (1–3, 9), contemporary events like the journey of Augustus to the Orient (4) or the victory of Actium (11) — the first as a contrast to the poet's love-life at home, the second essentially as a victory over Cleopatra, with whose power over Antony (comparable to that of a Medea and Omphale, Penthesilea and Semiramis) Propertius (as a poet) excuses his own bondage. Among other themes, there is praise of Italy (22), the death of a young friend (7) and the death of Marcellus (18). Even erotic poems do not always refer to Cynthia. The Antiope legend (15), despite its moral for Cynthia, jealous of her lady's maid, is told essentially for its own sake.

Book II was published after the death of Cornelius Gallus (26 B.C.); book III must fall in the years between the death of Marcellus (23 B.C.) and the return of the Roman standards taken by the Parthians (20 B.C.).

Book IV shows Propertius changed: he is now a Roman Callimachus, anticipating Ovid's *Fasti*. The old god Vertumnus, whose statue stood in Vicus Tuscus, introduces himself (2); we hear of the temple of Palatine Apollo erected in thanksgiving for the victory of Actium (6), of the *Ara Maxima* of Hercules (9), of Iuppiter Feretrius and the *spolia opima* of Romulus, A. Cornelius Cossus and M. Claudius Marcellus (10): the Tarpeia story (4) gives Propertius the chance to apply his skill in erotic psychology to a Roman legend. The remaining elegies of the book have nothing to do with patriotic themes. They are, however, quite different from his earlier love poetry. There is the *lena* (5), an authentic comedy figure, who advises a young woman in matters of love; when she urges her to value gold more than charming words, Propertius ironically makes her quote his own lines to Cynthia. In another poem (8) he describes, not without humour, how Cynthia once went to Lanuvium, with another man, and he himself invited two girls; but Cynthia came back unexpectedly and there was a stormy scene. In the moving seventh poem the dead Cynthia appears to her former lover in a dream; the bitterness has given way to a gentle sadness. The most mature poems are 3 and 11. The letter of Arethusa to her husband on the battlefield is a masterly self-portrayal of a woman's mind. Ovid attempted something similar in his *Heroides*, but he neither sought nor achieved the depth of Propertius. Also the last poem (11), words of consolation of the dead Cornelia to her husband, is above all a self-portrait of a loving wife; the human appeal of this gentle woman and the tone of muted sadness have earned this poem the title of *regina elegiarum*.

The latest contemporary allusions in book IV (departure of Augustus for Gaul and the consulate of Cornelia's brother P. Cornelius Scipio) refer to the year 16 B.C. After this we hear of the poet no more.

Propertius made a powerful impression on his contemporaries as well as on posterity. Ovid listened with enthusiasm to his recitations; his fellow countryman and disciple Passenus Paulus wrote elegies in the Propertian manner a century after the poet's death; Lucan and Martial bear witness to his popularity; Propertian lines are found even on the walls of Pompeii. His influence on poetic language lasts to the end of antiquity. To the middle ages Propertius, in contrast to the sententious Ovid, meant but little; not until the Renaissance, beginning with Petrarch, was he newly discovered.

P. OVIDIUS NASO

The last of the elegiac poets, Ovid, stands on the threshold of a new era. Born only a few years after Propertius, he belongs nevertheless to another generation. As a poet he consciously follows the tradition which started with Gallus; but he did not devote himself to elegy as exclusively as did his predecessors. Prolific and versatile in his almost effortless production, he not only found new modes of expression and created a new style; he is altogether a *modern* poet, his work is the prototype of Romance literature.

Ovid speaks more often and more personally about himself

than any other poet of his time. His autobiography in *Tristia* IV, 10, is remarkable for its wealth of factual and psychological detail. He was born on 20th March, 43 B.C., in Sulmo in the country of the Paeligni. His father was then already over forty years old. As the son of a well-to-do family of equestrian rank, Ovid was destined for a public career. He studied rhetoric in Rome, where Porcius Latro and Arellius Fuscus were his teachers. As a *declamator* he favoured the *suasoria*; of the *controversiae* he loved only those which called for the portrayal of human character; to argue a case was not in his line. Already then he felt irresistibly drawn towards poetry, which rather displeased his matter-of-fact father. As was then customary, the young Ovid broadened his education through travel; for some time he stayed in Athens. At eighteen he was already giving public recitations of his poems; the Corinna elegies, he says, were soon on everybody's lips. Messalla took the young poet into his circle; but for Ovid, who could afford to live independently, this did not mean to be tied to a patron. He soon resigned public office, for which he had no inclination, and gave himself wholly to the enjoyment of a refined life and to his beloved poetry. He married young, but his first and second marriages soon ended in divorce; only in his third wife did he find the right companion. He lived with her in a happy, harmonious marriage; he was father of one daughter, who while still young gave him two grandchildren; he was the centre of a congenial circle of friends, and already a celebrated poet. Apart from his love of poetry he had composed a tragedy, the *Medea*, he was working on a poetic calendar of Rome, the *Fasti*, and was just on the point of finishing the *Metamorphoses*.

Then, suddenly, fate struck: in A.D. 8, he was banished by Augustus to the farthest boundaries of the empire, the barely civilized Tomi on the Black Sea, open to raids by the neighbouring barbarians. The cause of his relegation was, as Ovid says, *carmen et error* (*Trist.* II, 207). About the *carmen* there can be little doubt: it was probably the *Ars amatoria*, that all too knowledgeable, all too outspoken book on free love. On its very appearance (about 1 B.C.) it incurred Augustus's displeasure; from then on the poet was on a black list. The *error*, the direct occasion of his banishment, would seem to be Ovid's having become an accessory in a scandal which concerned Augustus personally, perhaps in the adultery of his granddaughter, the younger Julia. The effect of the punishment on the fifty-one-year-old Ovid was shattering. He left Rome towards the end of the year. His wife wanted to follow him into exile, but on his urgent request stayed behind in Rome; she fought to the last for his pardon, but without success. Even Ovid's works were removed from the public libraries.

After a long journey, made harder by the winter, Ovid reached Tomi in the spring of A.D. 9. It took years before the gentle and witty Ovid, used to comfort and stimulating company, began to settle down there. But he adapted himself to his new life better than he had thought. He allowed the *Metamorphoses* to be published without giving them the final touch (he had thrown his work into the fire when he heard the imperial decree, but copies were already in the hands of friends). For the continuation of the *Fasti*, which were half finished, he lacked the antiquarian material. Yet he could not stop writing verse. The poetry of those years (five books of *Tristia*, four books *Ex Ponto*) shows a gradual change from complaints, attempts at justification, pleas to his wife and friends to work for his return, from bitter contrasts of the past and present and gloomy accounts of his exile, to a certain interest in his new environment. Ovid took part in the defence of the town against barbarian attacks, he learnt the language of the natives and even wrote poetry in it. He never gave up his hopes of return; they were revived once more when, after Augustus's death, Germanicus, the nephew of the emperor Tiberius, himself a gifted poet, went to the East in A.D. 17. Ovid dedicated to him the six books of the *Fasti* which he had brought with him from Rome, and which he was now beginning to revise. There is, however, no evidence of a revision beyond the first book; he probably died before his task was completed. Tomi (now Constanza, in Rumania) has honoured the banished poet as its greatest citizen to the present day.

Ovid's earliest poetry was love elegies (*Amores*) in the manner of his friends Tibullus and Propertius. The *Heroides* too, love-letters written by women of Greek saga to their absent husbands or lovers, had antecedents in earlier elegy, but were first established as a literary form by Ovid. The same is true of his 'Art of Love': a didactic poem, which in metre as well as in style and spirit is elegiac. The 'Remedies for love' (*Remedia amoris*) is a counterpart to the 'Art of Love'. A poem on cosmetics (*De medicamine faciei*) survives incomplete.

The *Fasti* are an elegiac cycle after the manner of Callimachus. The feasts of the Roman year with their customs and legends were to be told in the order of the calendar, but Ovid only completed the first half of the work.

The *Metamorphoses* also are a cycle of tales; but here Ovid has endeavoured to turn the cyclic poem into an epic. He links the individual stories together in a 'chronological' sequence, which extends from the creation of the world to the apotheosis of Caesar. As an epic, the poem is in hexameters.

From his exile, Ovid wrote the *Tristia* and the letters *Ex Ponto*. The elegy here becomes a purely personal message. Some masterpieces apart, one feels that Ovid's poetic powers are on the decline. In Tomi, Ovid also wrote the elegy *Ibis*, an invective, full of dark curses, against an enemy in Rome, and (probably) the didactic poem on fish and fishing (*Halieutica*), which has remained a fragment.

Even the earliest poetry of Ovid is rhetorical, and his poetry remained rhetorical to the end of his life. For Ovid this is an aesthetic principle; rhetoric and poetry spring from the same source and enrich one another. But this rhetoric is guided by psychological insight. The *Amores*, which on the whole are only brilliant variations on familiar themes, contain also some pieces of a strong human appeal, *e.g.* the lover's longing for his beloved while being away from her at the country home (II, 16); the lament over the death of Tibullus (III, 9); the story, almost Propertian in character, of the midday visit of Corinna (I, 5), or the Aurora poem (I, 13). By and large, however, Ovid's outspoken eroticism does not always compensate for lesser intensity of feeling. It is significant that the sorrow of love has no room in these poems. Whether Corinna was a real woman is hard to say; it has been remarked with some reason that the real heroine of the *Amores* is Elegy.

The *Heroides*, like the Arethusa letter of Propertius and, in a different way, his questions addressed to Cynthia's slave Lygdamus, raise a rhetorical exercise, namely, to write in an assumed or fictitious character, to the status of art. This practice must have been congenial to Ovid's talent. The poetic love-letter already existed in hellenism. Ovid here shows himself a sympathetic interpreter of the female psyche; he humanizes mythology more thoroughly than did even Euripides or Apollonios Rhodios.

The *Ars amatoria*, in three books, is despite its elegiac form a parody of a didactic poem. Books on the art of love were as well known in classical antiquity as they still are in the Orient; the theme was taken up also by Tibullus (*e.g.* I, 4) and Propertius (IV, 5). Here too Ovid created something original: themes of the love elegy, subjective and mythological, are combined with a profusion of subtle observations; not until the end does the 'art of love' become a technique of love.

Of all Ovid's works the fifteen books of *Metamorphoses* have had the greatest and most lasting influence. Many generations have learnt from this work the myths and legends of antiquity; more than all other books of ancient poetry they have stimulated literature and fine arts up to the Renaissance. Within Ovid's work they hold a special place, on the borderline of elegiac and heroic poetry. This is most clearly seen when they are contrasted with the *Fasti* (of the same period), because some tales (*e.g.*

the Proserpina legend) are told in both works. That Ovid himself considered the *Metamorphoses* as his masterpiece is shown by the proud epilogue (XV, 871 ff.). The transformation of human beings into other shapes is a universal theme. In antiquity there were many stories especially of people changing into birds; such stories had been collected by an older friend of Ovid, Aemilius Macer, in his *Ornithogonia*. In hellenism, with its interest in astrology, legends setting human beings among the stars were popular. Nicander of Colophon (third or second century B.C.) had written *Heteroioumena* ('transformations') in hexameters and Parthenius had composed *Metamorphoses* in elegiac metre. Ovid, however, was the first to have the idea (which would have seemed monstrous to a Greek) not only to bind together so many stories of transformations in a cycle, but also to set them in a chronological framework in which the age of the gods, that of the heroes and that of the great men of history, are the main epochs. For detail, Ovid is of course indebted to all literature which had treated any of his stories before him: epic and tragedy, epyllion and prose tale, Pythagorean teaching (as philosophical foundation for the principle of metamorphosis) and antiquarian research. How cleverly he made use of all that he had taken over is shown, *inter alia*, in his story of Philemon and Baucis (VIII, 618 ff.), basically a Phrygian folk legend, which was still alive at the time of the apostle Paul. With all his rhetoric (which the ancient reader, unlike us, did not regard as artificial) Ovid becomes in the *Metamorphoses* a great narrator; he is as successful in the grand manner as he is in an idyllic or comic vein. Stories like those of Niobe or Medea are tensely dramatic, and the speeches of his characters are often distinguished by psychological subtlety or tragic pathos. Love in all its forms (Narcissus, Pygmalion) is a principal theme. Ovid displays special skill in the description of the process of transformation. His main interest, however, is in the portrayal of human nature; even his gods (unlike those of Homer or Vergil) are drawn purely as human beings.

In *Tristia* (A.D. 9–12) and *Ex Ponto* (A.D. 12–16) Ovid resumes the poetic forms of his earlier period. Some poems, *e.g.* his farewell to Rome (*Trist.* I, 3), the impressions of the Scythian winter and spring (III, 10 and 12), or the autobiography (IV, 10), still have connexions with the great elegiac tradition. But the majority bore us by their continual complaining and by the poet's self-abasement in misfortune.

Poems on Augustus and Tiberius are lost, among them one in the Getic language. The surviving *Ibis* was modelled on the poem of the same name of Callimachus. The *Halieutica* is a didactic poem in the narrow, technical sense like the hunting poem (*Cynegetica*) of Grattius, which Ovid (*Pont.* IV, 16, 34) mentions and of which over five hundred lines are surviving.

Even Ovid's contemporaries saw clearly the merits and weaknesses of his poetry. The elder Seneca, who often heard him declaim, said that he knew his own faults, but was fond of them (*non ignoravit vitia sua, sed amavit*). Quintilian was of the same opinion as Seneca: of *Medea* he said it showed what the poet might have achieved had he mastered his talent instead of yielding to it. One must agree with this judgement in all essentials. Side by side with incredible smoothness of language and verse-construction, superb skill in the overcoming of technical difficulties and an astonishing talent of giving his borrowings an original turn, there is a certain carelessness in workmanship. In the course of prolonged reading, moreover, the monotony of thoughts, themes, and effects rather palls on us. Ovid exhausts the possibilities of his themes — love-scenes, transformations, complaints about his banishment — all too thoroughly. His art lacks both greatness and profundity; its appeal is due largely to the poet's personal qualities — his refined *humanitas*, his psychological insight, his warm feelings for his wife and friends — which are evident in all his work.

Strange as it may seem, this poet was a favourite of the middle ages, almost as much as Vergil. It was certainly above all his technical virtuosity which recommended him as a model; given

some talent, he was the easiest to copy. The Ovidians of the
twelfth century show indeed an astonishing formal perfection.
They did not even take offence at Ovid's immorality. In
literature since the Renaissance an Ovidian tradition exists
alongside the Vergilian : *e.g.* Boccaccio as against Tasso.

Elegies were also written by minor poets under the influence
of the great masters. The pseudo-Vergilian Maecenas elegies
and book III of the Tibullus Corpus (for the greater part not
written by him) are cases in point. Under Ovid's name, though
falsely, go a *Consolatio ad Liviam* (occasioned by the death of
Prince Drusus) and the elegy *Nux* (The Nut-tree). The elegiac
form was cultivated in late antiquity by Christians no less than
by non-Christians. Even the theme of the classical love-elegy
experienced a short revival in the poetry of the Etruscan
Maximianus in the sixth century. His elegies are the work of
an elderly man looking back in a melancholy mood on the joys
of his youth—not without qualms of conscience, for Maximianus
was a Christian.

5. The Silver Age

A.D. 14–117

THE literature of the time between the death of Augustus (A.D. 14) and the ascent of Hadrian to the throne (A.D. 117) is overshadowed by a great past which was already recognized as classical. This is equally true of writers who followed the old patterns, varying and exhausting their possibilities, as did the majority, and of those who rejected them like Seneca and Lucan. The two stimuli to which Roman literature owed its life — creative imitation of the Greeks and self-expression in the adapted forms — had almost spent themselves. Such forms as the fable or the novel, which were coming into their own, belong to the less elevated spheres of literature; of established genres only the miniature art of the epigram now reaches perfection. The Greeks, whom Horace recommended to be read day and night, cease to be the decisive force in the shaping of Roman literature.

Literary output increased, and technical ability was considerable, but even works of great merit would no longer hold a central place in the nation's life. The mixing of styles progressed and the sway of rhetoric increased. Emperors like Nero and Domitian took a lively interest in literature; but poetical competitions *sub auspiciis principis* are not always a blessing. On the other hand, modern criticism of Silver Latin literature has rarely done it justice. This period not only brought forth a number of remarkable individuals in the world of letters, but also some of the most impressive works of Roman literature. It is not until then that Roman historiography attained to its solitary climax in the work of Tacitus.

Oratory, which under Augustus had stood its ground with difficulty, now meets its inevitable doom. Among the orators of his time Quintilian places only Domitius Afer from Nemausus (Nîmes) beside the ancients. In Southern Gaul, from whence he came, a rhetorical tradition grew up which was to take the lead in the third century. Tacitus, whose father-in-law Agricola had studied in Massilia (Marseilles), bears witness to the intellectual life of that city. Soon, however, the art of oratory was to become mere rhetoric for its own sake. Partly as panegyric, partly as declamation, it attracted a wide public even outside the schools.

To be born in such a time was the tragedy of the greatest teacher of Roman eloquence, M. FABIUS QUINTILIANUS from Calagurris in Spain (approx. A.D. 35-95). Brought up in Rome, then a teacher in his home town, he was brought back to the capital by Galba when he became emperor (A.D. 68). Vespasian appointed him as the first public professor of rhetoric; Domitian entrusted to him the education of his great-nephews and honoured him with a consulship. His principal work, the twelve books of *Institutio oratoria*, is a course of oratorical training in the framework of a comprehensive educational and cultural programme. It is based on wide knowledge of theory and a mature personal judgement of the poetry and prose of the Greeks and Romans; but above all the author draws on the experience of his own practice as an orator and teacher. Against the abuses of rhetoric and against Seneca's fashionable aphoristic style, he points indefatigably to Cicero as the great model; on him he also modelled his own style, with considerable success. He was not blind to the decline of his art; this is shown by his earlier essay *De causis corruptae eloquentiae*. He seems to have put the blame mainly on the neglect of the classical models; the real causes, which were inherent in the political and cultural situation, he could not or would not see.

The writing of history shared the fate of oratory: partiality for the republic, or criticism of the *princeps* or his favourites, could be dangerous for the author. A. CREMUTIUS CORDUS, who under Augustus had written on the beginnings of the principate, was accused as an admirer of Brutus and Cassius in A.D. 25; he died by starving himself to death. His *Annales* were condemned to be burned; they were, however, circulated secretly, and his daughter Marcia later published them in an expurgated form. On the other hand, the Germanic wars of AUFIDIUS BASSUS and his imperial history seem to have met with no objection. C. VELLEIUS PATERCULUS, probably from Capua, composed for the consul of A.D. 30, M. Vinicius, a synopsis in two books of Roman history up to this year. The title is lost with the beginning of the work. Velleius has value as a contemporary historian of the early principate, the only one who has come down to us; he is, *inter alia*, an important source for the history of Germany at the beginning of our era. His rhetorical style (which, however, cannot make us forget the haste in which he had to write) outdoes itself in hyperbolic expressions referring to Tiberius. It is the style which we still use when addressing royalty. But the admiration of the officer for his commander-in-chief is genuine, and the account of what he personally witnessed is vivid and effective. The historical *exempla* (*Factorum et dictorum memorabilium libri novem*) of VALERIUS MAXIMUS rank considerably lower; they were published soon after the fall of Seianus (A.D. 31) and dedicated to Tiberius.

Much safer than history were the technical disciplines. Under Tiberius and Claudius, Q. REMMIUS PALAEMON from Vicenza was important as a grammarian. Of low birth, self-taught and incredibly conceited, he wrote a comprehensive *Ars grammatica* which was much used until the end of antiquity. At about the beginning of Nero's reign, Q. ASCONIUS PEDIANUS wrote against Vergil's critics and composed historical comments on Cicero's orations. Geographical interest, awakened by Agrippa's map of the empire, had created a market for the *Chorographia* of the Spaniard POMPONIUS MELA. He probably wrote under Claudius. Without personal research, yet drawing on good sources, the educated author composed a concise but stimulating work in the fashionable style of the time. Also under Claudius L. IUNIUS MODERATUS COLUMELLA from Gades wrote a comprehensive treatise in twelve books on agriculture. He brought to his task love of nature and enthusiasm for his subject. Columella, who wrote a careful prose style (and in book X, on gardening, pleasing hexameters), gave his discipline the canonical form for centuries to come, and recorded many interesting details of contemporary social and economic life.

In the second half of the century falls the activity of the officer and engineer SEX. IULIUS FRONTINUS, who was twice consul and in A.D. 97 *curator aquarum*. As such he wrote, originally for his own instruction, a commentary on Rome's water supply (*De aquis urbis Romae*), which he later published in deference to the wish of Trajan. It is the best technical work in the Latin language. To his military interest we owe the three books on stratagems (*Strategemata*; a fourth book is probably not by him). He also wrote on land-surveying.

Encyclopaedic literature also flourished. Of the extensive Encyclopaedia of A. CORNELIUS CELSUS (under Tiberius), who wrote, among other things, on husbandry, the art of war, oratory, law and philosophy, only eight books *De medicina* survive: the work of a well-read layman, who knows how to report in pure language and in a well-controlled style.

A considerable number of subjects are surveyed in the *Naturalis Historia* of the elder Pliny (C. PLINIUS SECUNDUS) from Comum, who had a successful military and civil career (A.D. 50/51 with Pomponius Secundus in lower Germany, A.D. 70, on the General Staff of Titus at Jerusalem, then procurator of Syria). As commander of the fleet of Misenum he lost his life at the eruption of Vesuvius in A.D. 79. As well as a work on cavalry tactics (*De iaculatione equestri*) and a grammatical work (*Dubii sermonis libri VIII*) he wrote a monograph on Rome's German wars and a history of his own time. There survive only the thirty-seven books of his *Natural History*, in which he writes of cosmology, geography, anthropology, zoology, botany (including *materia medica*) and mineralogy. In his philosophy (a vague stoicism) uncritical belief in authority is mixed with scepticism, science with superstition; but despite all lack of method, factual errors and stylistic mannerisms, this gigantic compilation, which was much studied in the middle ages and in the Renaissance, is an invaluable source for many aspects of ancient life.

In poetry the most original author is PHAEDRUS, a freedman of Augustus. His *Fabulae Aesopiae* were published in five books under Tiberius, Caligula and Claudius. Fables were known in Rome as everywhere; even poets like Ennius, Lucilius and Horace had made use of them. But a *book* of fables was something new. Besides Aesopian fables in the narrower sense, we find anecdotes (mostly from Greek sources), and even pieces of the poet's own invention. The proletarian, which he remained despite his rhetorical education, saw in the moralizing fable a means of telling the powerful people of his time the truth in a veiled form. Even this he did not always do with impunity, as he implies in his prologues and epilogues. Phaedrus's language and style are simple and natural except when he is moralizing; he has a tendency towards strong and direct expression; there is also, as might be expected, occasional parody. As verse he chose a slightly antiquated metre, the popular *Senarius*. Recognition was denied him in his lifetime; Seneca seems to ignore him deliberately. The first to mention him is Martial; his fame begins in late antiquity. Of that time date some prose adaptations of his fables, of which the 'Romulus' (fifth century) is best known. From here an uninterrupted tradition leads to the fable-writers of the middle ages and to the literary fable of the moderns (La Fontaine).

Most epic poets of the period are content with trying to develop new possibilities of the traditional forms. GERMANI-CUS, the nephew and adopted son of Tiberius, attempted a free translation of Aratus; it shows formal ability and a certain poetic talent. New ground was covered by one M. MANILIUS, about whose person nothing is known — he seems to have written in the early years of Tiberius — with his five books of *Astronomica*. As truly a poet as was Lucretius, Manilius makes astrology, conceived in the spirit of stoicism, the theme of his epic. The creative powers for which so intractable a subject would call are in evidence not only in the mythological and philosophical digressions but even in purely technical sections.

Vergil had taken the heroic epic to a height which seemed unattainable even to his contemporaries; a later generation saw in the *Aeneid* a challenge that was better evaded. The first to do so was the nephew of Seneca the philosopher, M. ANNAEUS LUCANUS. The subject of his epic *Pharsalia* (in ten books) was the civil war between Pompey and Caesar. A stoic like Seneca, he chose Pompey for his hero; this was a mistake, not only historically but also artistically. If Vergil had shown the Roman present in the mirror of a mythical past, Lucan continued the earlier tradition of the Roman epic, which told contemporary history directly. But while Ennius and his followers, in the Homeric manner, made the gods actively intervene, Lucan broke with his epic tradition. Whether this had anything to do with his stoic theology or not, it certainly was justifiable on artistic grounds. Lucan strives to impress above all by elaborate descriptions and speeches, but also by poignant aphorisms. The rhetorical pathos, if often excessive, is always sincere. In spite of its republican spirit and the harsh criticism with which it met on aesthetic grounds, the poem proved a great success. Some epic poets of the later first century were under Lucan's influence. As a school-book, the *Pharsalia* was often commented on in later antiquity and the middle ages.

From before the eruption of Vesuvius in A.D. 79, perhaps still from the later Augustan era, dates a *Carmen de bello Actiaco*, of which about seventy lines have survived. The poet seems to have followed the conventions with which Lucan broke: Atropos, one of the Fates, is introduced as the invisible witness of the suicide plans of Cleopatra. Another way of getting round the *Aeneid* was the epic treatment of Greek legends. The earliest surviving epics of this kind belong to the Flavian era: the *Argonautica* of C. VALERIUS FLACCUS (the passage which alludes to the conquest of Jerusalem must have been written in about A.D. 70) and the *Thebais* and *Achilleis* of Statius. The incomplete (or incompletely surviving) *Argonautica* are modelled on the epic of the same name by the Alexandrian Apollonius of Rhodes, but with great freedom in the treatment of the subject; whilst Apollonius likes to display his learning, the Roman poet, who has learned from Vergil and Ovid, leans more strongly on the psychology of his characters. A greater poet was P. PAPINIUS STATIUS from Naples. His father introduced him as a boy to the study of the poets; he himself showed unusual poetic talent early in his youth and won prizes in poetry competitions. In Rome he recited successfully from his *Thebais*. He lived in a childless but happy marriage with a widow named Claudia. Later he went back to Naples; he died probably in A.D. 96. The fame and influence of Statius rest on his epic *Thebais* in twelve books. His main subject is the campaign of the Seven against Thebes. The first three books, however, tell in detail the antecedents of the expedition; the last book tells of the appeal of the Argive women to Athens and its result. Even in the body of the work the composition is loose, but a unifying motif is provided by the curse of Oedipus. A turning aside from the classical spirit is seen (as also in Seneca's drama) in the poet's taste for the gruesome on one side, for the pathetic on the other. But despite the often overburdened and affected language and a surfeit of similes, the work is impressive. Much simpler in style is the completed portion of *Achilleis*. It stops in the middle of the second book, on the departure of Achilles to Troy. The most elaborated episode is the stay of Achilles, disguised as a girl, on the island of Scyros. In the last years of Statius fall his *Silvae*. They are a collection of occasional poems (mostly dactylic, but also in lyric metres) ; for the greater part, they were written on commission, for persons of the emperor's entourage, on whom Statius was in some degree dependent, but also for other distinguished friends : descriptions of their villas, baths and art treasures, congratulations and poetic necrologues. This is all very ably done but is interesting mainly as a contribution to the social history of the Flavian era. Only rarely, as in the moving *Somnus*, does the poet speak personally. While the *Silvae* were as good as forgotten in the middle ages, both epics were eagerly read. Even for Dante, Statius is almost equal to Vergil.

In the later years of Domitian were also written the seventeen books of *Punica* by SILIUS ITALICUS. Nero's last consul A.D. 68, then proconsul of Asia, he lived in honoured retirement, without influence, but also without enemies, on his lovely estates, worshipping the past. He acquired Cicero's Tusculanum ; his estate at Naples included Vergil's grave. There he died (probably in A.D. 101) from a painful tumor ; he bore his suffering with composure and preserved to the last day his serenity of mind. Patriotism and enthusiasm for Rome's heroic age seem to have inspired his epic, on which he worked from about A.D. 80. It is, one might almost say, emphatically conservative : the epic *comme il faut*. The story of the war with Hannibal, told essentially after Livy, yet seasoned with exquisite antiquarian learning, presents itself as a pageant, parading all the Homeric-Vergilian paraphernalia. Language and verse-construction are regular to the point of monotony. If Silius knew the *Annales* of Ennius, he might have seen in this epic the justification for his own treatment of the subject. But Ennius was a great poet.

The eclogues of T. CALPURNIUS SICULUS from the beginning of the reign of Nero and the approximately contemporary anonymous poems (*Laus Pisonis* and two *Bucolica*) show that bucolic poetry was already beginning to lose its aesthetic *raison d'être*. Several poems, like other literature of the time, praise Nero, on whom in those years great hope was placed; in this court-poetry the shepherds are little more than masks. The poems of Calpurnius are followed in the manuscripts by four eclogues of NEMESIANUS from Carthage, probably of the third century, who is also the author of a hunting poem (*Cynegetica*). The third eclogue with its Bacchic scenes is one of the finest poems of later antiquity.

Quintilian mentions as a lyric poet one CAESIUS BASSUS; he seems to have met his death at the eruption of Vesuvius of A.D. 79. Persius, who was a friend of his, dedicated to him his sixth satire (see below). Bassus also wrote on metre; he taught, after Varro, that all metres derive from the hexameter and trimeter. This work survives in part.

The value of the six satires of the short-lived A. PERSIUS FLACCUS (A.D. 34-62) is disputed: the great admiration in antiquity and the middle ages has given way in more recent times to a rather critical attitude. He came from an Etruscan family of equestrian status in Volaterrae; after the early death of his father he was brought up by his mother; he became a disciple and inseparable friend of the stoic Annaeus Cornutus, who probably introduced him to the stoic opposition against Nero (Paetus Thrasea and Seneca); he was a model son and brother, gentle and of almost maidenly modesty. The fact that quite a different picture of the poet would seem to emerge from his satires is due to Persius's close imitation of his models (Lucilius and Horace). Apart from the literary criticism of the first satire, his themes are taken from the stoic diatribe, enlivened with elements of the mime. Persius's language often approaches the colloquial; on the other hand he carries the aphoristic tendency of his time to extremes. But between expanses of calculated obscurity, we encounter passages which reveal great talent.

The satire of a certain SULPICIA purports to date from the

time of Domitian. It complains about the expulsion of the philosophers by the emperor and prophesies his early death. For a long time it was thought that this Sulpicia was the erotic poetess of that name, who lived about that time, but most scholars now see in this poem a work of later date put into the mouth of that Sulpicia.

Only two authors of the Claudian era have found a permanent place in world literature: Seneca and Petronius.

L. ANNAEUS SENECA, a son of the rhetor, turned early to philosophy; he followed mainly the Cynics and Stoics. His public career began under Caligula, but Claudius banished him on the instigation of Messalina in A.D. 41; Claudius's last wife Agrippina, however, got a pardon for him in A.D. 49 and made him the tutor of her son Nero. Seneca at first had great influence on the young *princeps*; in A.D. 56 he was consul suffectus. In A.D. 55/56 he dedicated to Nero the three books *De clementia*, two of which survive. Later the two men became estranged and Seneca withdrew, disappointed, from the court. On account of his alleged participation in the Piso conspiracy he was forced to suicide by Nero in A.D. 65.

As a philosophical essayist and as a poet Seneca strongly impressed his contemporaries and influenced posterity. His development as a philosopher escapes our knowledge because many of his works cannot be dated with certainty; perhaps the cynic element was stronger at first, the humanized stoicism of Posidonius prevailed later; disappointment over Nero also left its mark. At that time more than ever stoicism was practised as a way of life in Rome. In this spirit Seneca tried to act as a guide to introspection and moral edification. Seneca deliberately wrote in the style of his time — tersely and pointedly, in contrast to Ciceronian periodizing; but he rather overdid it. This earned him the blame of the classicists and later of the archaists. Like Ovid he was too fond of his own mannerisms, with the same result: the effect would wear off.

Seneca's prose writing is concerned almost exclusively with practical moral philosophy. The twelve *Dialogi* (not platonic dialogues, but diatribes after the manner of Bion) include among other themes *De vita beata*, *De tranquillitate animi*, *De brevitate vitae*, *De ira* and *De otio*; three pieces are consolations (to Marcia, daughter of Cremutius Cordus; to Polybius, an influential court official of Claudius, and to his mother Helvia). Of a similar nature are the seven books *De beneficiis* and the 'Prince's Mirror', the *De clementia*. Even the seven books of the *Naturales quaestiones*, dedicated to his younger friend Lucilius, then procurator of Sicily, give wide scope to moral reflections. In the *Epistulae morales*, likewise dedicated to Lucilius, Seneca assumes openly the role of teacher and moral adviser.

Without discarding completely the moral values of ancient Rome, Seneca develops an introspective morality, which centres on the individual. He was among the first accurately to describe mental states (*e.g.* boredom: *Dial.* 9, 2). Modern, like his psychology, is also his humanism; it includes respect for the slave as a human being. Christianity saw in him a kindred spirit, even a secret Christian, and under his name invented a correspondence with the apostle Paul.

To stimulate moral responses is the principal aim also of Seneca's Tragedies. Nine plays are extant: *Hercules Oetaeus*, *Hercules furens*, *Troades*, *Phoenissae*, *Medea*, *Phaedra*, *Oedipus*, *Agamemnon* and *Thyestes*.[1] They all have parallels in Attic tragedy; it would seem, however, that Seneca's treatment of themes as well as of metres (in the choruses) owes much to the postclassical tragedy of the Greeks, and also to Augustan tragedy (Ovid's *Medea*). Typical of Seneca's tragic style is a very intensified pathos; plot and characterization are to him of comparatively lesser importance. Seneca does not strive after the Aristotelian catharsis, but after effects which are in the nature

---

[1] Under Seneca's name (wrongly, no doubt) goes also the play *Octavia*, the only surviving specimen of a *fabula praetexta*. Its subject is the sad fate of Nero's first wife.

of a moral shock. These tragedies, written in a strongly rhetorical vein, were primarily if not exclusively intended for recitation, as were those of his contemporaries. Yet Seneca, and not the tragedy of the Greeks, was the model for the classical drama of the French and Italians; Seneca even had a strong influence on the Elizabethan drama, particularly on Shakespeare. We should not forget this when we are inclined to find fault, but rather try to judge the dramatist on his own terms.

The most original work of Seneca is his *Ludus de morte Claudii*, called in the principal manuscript *Divi Claudii Apotheosis per saturam*, and most probably identical with the *Apocolocyntosis* mentioned by Cassius Dio. It is a parody of an apotheosis (*i.e.* of the deification of an emperor), and proceeds from the unedifying death scene of Claudius (officially already deified) up to his scornful reception and infamous fate in a comic underworld. Seneca, who had to write the official funeral speech for the hated ruler, here takes his posthumous revenge. It is certainly political satire, but not a political pamphlet; the work was intended for the circle of the young Nero. For this reason the satire is interrupted by a praise of the golden age which is to come with the new regime: on this point, for all his flattery, the author was sincere. The *Apocolocyntosis*, not only on account of its form (mixture of prose and verse), but also in style and motifs, is a *Satura Menippea*, the only one which survives complete.

No greater contrast to Seneca is imaginable than PETRONIUS ARBITER, author of a *Satiricon* in at least sixteen books. One may recognize in him that Petronius of whose life and character Tacitus gives so impressive a picture and whose death (ordered by Nero) he describes in deliberate contrast with that of Seneca. No one but the *elegantiae arbiter* at Nero's court has a better claim to the authorship of this unique work, so full of life even in its fragmentary state. A man of the highest culture and a *bon vivant*, he nevertheless discharged his duties very creditably as consul and as proconsul of Bithynia; but having shown the world how capable he was, he resumed his hedonistic life. At the court he set the tone in matters of taste and had Nero's confidence in all personal affairs. His rival Tigellinus finally brought about his downfall.

As a work of literature the *Satiricon* of Petronius is difficult to classify. In content, even down to individual situations, it is a parody of the *Odyssey*, but at the same time a parody of those novels in which lovers were unexpectedly separated and, after being proved in many adventures, were reunited. Petronius's lovers, however, are a young man and a handsome boy, Encolpius and Giton, and their frequent separation is the revenge of the obscene god Priapus, whom Encolpius (who tells his own story) had offended. As Poseidon hunts Odysseus across the seas, so Priapus chases Encolpius from one disgraceful adventure to another. One is often reminded of the 'Ulysses' of James Joyce, whom the author of the *Satiricon* matches in his masterly description of all aspects of life without discrimination, and also in the art of modulating his language over the widest imaginable range of speakers and subjects. The *Satiricon* is indebted also to diatribe (though not to its moralizing) and mime; elements of the latter are recognizable above all in the *Cena Trimalchionis*. This banquet of the *parvenu* Trimalchio and his friends, set in a provincial town in Southern Italy, allows us invaluable glimpses of the world of the advancing lower classes.

A novel of another sort, or something very near to a novel, is the Alexander history (*Historiae Alexandri Magni* in ten books) of the rhetor Q. CURTIUS RUFUS, who probably wrote under Claudius. His style is similar to that of Seneca. As popular reading, for which the work was intended, it fulfilled its purpose. Together with the Alexander novel of Iulius Valerius (fifth century) it became the source of a masterpiece of mediaeval Latin literature, the *Alexandreis* of Walter of Châtillon in the twelfth century.

The history of manners of the Flavian era, especially of the time of Domitian, unfolds before us in the epigrams of the contemporary Martial, and a generation later in the satires of Juvenal.

M. VALERIUS MARTIALIS came from Bilbilis in Tarragonian Spain. His years of manhood (about A.D. 64–98) were spent in Rome. It was not for him to work for a living; he preferred to struggle as a man of letters and hanger-on of the great. In this he must have been quite successful: he later owned a town house and a small country estate and had sufficient means to become a knight. He paid for his success with the prostitution of his art. He incessantly praised the tyrant Domitian as the ideal ruler; when, under Nerva, the wind had changed, Martial attempted a *volte-face*. This time he seems to have had no luck; he returned to Bilbilis a little apprehensive as to how he would be received. He died there between A.D. 102 and A.D. 104.

Martial cultivated one poetic form only, the epigram. In this art he certainly had predecessors; he himself names among others Catullus and Domitius Marsus, whose *Cicuta* ('drink of hemlock') was perhaps his model for using the epigram as a form of satire. But it was also quite in the spirit of the time that a poet like Martial, whose strength lay in the acute observation of his environment and in the gift for pointed expression, should dedicate himself exclusively to a minor form of art, which in a certain sense was a counterpart to the aphorism of Seneca. Martial collected his (more than fifteen hundred) epigrams into books, which he edited individually or in groups, many with a preface in verse or prose. The books are of mixed content: literature, society, and personal matters. Martial's silence concerning Tacitus and Statius is noteworthy. He doubtless regarded the latter as a rival for patronage. He depicts the society of his time as a shrewd observer but with moral indifference; his mockery, often hurtful, is not born of indignation. The obscene pieces (and of these there are not a few) are rather boring variations on a few themes. In the personal poems despicable flattery and calculating complaints about his 'poverty' take up much space; but we also read such charming pieces as his 'justification' before the serious Quintilian (II, 90). Among his metres, the Catullan hendecasyllable and the choliambic are still frequent, but the elegiac couplet predominates. The variation of metres within one book is as skilful as is that of the themes· Technically (and this includes the formulation of ideas) Martial brought the epigram to its highest perfection and often even exceeded the Greeks in wit and bite. To the present day he has remained the classic of the epigram.

D. IUNIUS IUVENALIS, from Aquinum in the land of the Volsci, first began to write in the time of Trajan. He was already middle-aged; earlier he had been a rhetor, and Martial knows him only as such. He was born at the latest in A.D. 67 and was still alive in A.D. 127.

The sixteen satires of Juvenal were published by the author in five successive books as we still read them. In his style effective rhetorical pathos combined with a liveliness which points beyond Horace to Lucilius; but he has neither the seignorial nonchalance of the one nor the cultured humanity of the other. A certain casualness of language, roughness of verse construction, and a looseness of composition might be intentional.

Juvenal is an 'activist'. Art is for him a representation of the topical, of unadorned reality. He therefore gives the satire priority over all the 'idealizing' poetic forms. As a *castigator morum* ('critic of morals'), to which he limits the function of the satirist, he passes judgement on the vices of the time or more exactly on the vices of Rome's high society. The standard of his criticism is not a moral philosophy, but the conventional conservative morals of a provincial. Still, his indignation is genuine, though we should guard against accepting his picture of the moral situation as representative even of the Roman upper class. According to his own artistic principle, he must describe actual incidents; but in the interest of effect, literary as well as moral, he must generalize. As a result, his victims, almost always real people (though of a bygone generation), act as timeless models of human depravity. The old, old theme of the bad woman becomes an unforgettable parade of Roman female types; so with tyrannical wives, blue-stockings, hypocritical bigots, and poisoners, to name but a few. The nightmare of life in the great city, the activity of would-be poets, homosexuality and prostitution, the sad plight of the intellectual, the helplessness of civilians against the guards — all is set before us in sharply observed miniature portraits. In his old age Juvenal's descriptive ability considerably declined, and little is left beyond declamatory invective (*e.g.* in *Sat.* 10). Juvenal was always sententious; scarcely any other work of similarly small extent (about four thousand lines) has so many quotable verses. The middle ages treasured him as a didactic moralist.

That Juvenal was able to describe the age of Domitian so bluntly shows that with Nerva and Trajan the pressure of despotism had weakened. The younger Pliny (C. PLINIUS CAECILIUS SECUNDUS) says so in his *Panegyricus*, the speech of thanksgiving to Trajan for his appointment to the consulship in A.D. 101. He was born in Comum, the home town of the Plinii. He studied under Quintilian. At the eruption of Vesuvius in A.D. 79 he was eighteen years old. The elder Pliny, who met his death in this catastrophe, had adopted his nephew in his will. Several inscriptions inform us of the public career of the younger Pliny, which culminated in his governorship of Bithynia (A.D. 111/12 or 112/13). Perhaps before his return, or certainly soon after, Pliny died. The nine books of *Epistulae*, on which his fame as an author rests, are literary letters: that is, the majority, although written to friends, were even then intended for later publication; this is shown not only by their careful form, but also by the limitation of each to one subject and by the use of certain rhetorical devices. Before their publication (probably in groups of books) Pliny added the finishing touch; at that stage perhaps he inserted some short letters of an epigrammatic character. The letters are not arranged chronologically, but on the principle of variation. In content they give a masterly picture of the society of the Trajanic era, as the *Silvae* of Statius and the epigrams of Martial do for the time of the Flavians. Pliny reveals himself in his letters as a distinguished and broadminded man, if not free from vanity ; we get to know him as a lawyer and official, as an owner of villas and a man of letters, as a benefactor of his native town in which he established a richly endowed library, and as a friend of men as different as Silius Italicus and Tacitus. But after so much charming small talk, it is refreshing to read the official correspondence with Trajan, which was added posthumously to his collected letters. The concise answers of the emperor to the requests for instruction by his meticulous subordinate make no pretence to literary attainment; but there we find what is lacking in Pliny — a great personality.

If we see in Pliny's friend P. CORNELIUS TACITUS Rome's greatest historian, the personality of the writer warrants this judgement no less than the special historical situation in which he wrote. He is indebted to the earlier historians of the principate not only for much of his material, but also for some of his interpretations; but he tests and selects, he goes back to the original sources (decrees of the senate, reports of generals and governors), and from the experience of his own time he forms a personal (and therefore necessarily subjective) view of history which by means of every possible literary device, he almost forces on the reader.

In the case of Tacitus life and work form as close a unity as in Cicero's. Son of a high official (his father was probably procurator of Belgium), yet hardly a descendent of the old *gens Cornelia* (one of his ancestors might have been granted citizenship by a Cornelian), Tacitus studied rhetoric and soon distinguished himself as an orator and lawyer. His public career began under Vespasian. During his praetorship (A.D. 88) he took part in the secular games of Domitian. When his father-in-law

Agricola died (A.D. 93) he was absent on an official mission away from Rome. He too experienced (*Agr.* 45) the crippling effect which the despotic regime of Domitian had on the mind and character of a gifted person; he did not begin to write until after Domitian's death. His relief, however, is mixed with bitterness for having spent the best years of his life in forced silence. Under Nerva, Tacitus was consul (A.D. 97); under Trajan, proconsul of Asia. His life seems to have extended into the reign of Hadrian, but the year of his death is unknown.

Pliny praises Tacitus's oratory as grandiose and solemn; he was famous for the address which as consul he delivered in memory of Verginius Rufus, the victor over the usurper Vindex. In his *Dialogus de oratoribus* he gives proof not only of rhetorical experience but also of deep insight into the conditions in which alone his profession was able to thrive.

At the peak of his fame as an orator, Tacitus turned to history. In A.D. 98 he published the biography of his father-in-law (*De vita et moribus Agricolae*) and soon after, in the same year, his *Germania*. The practice of oratory satisfied him less and less. His *Dialogus de oratoribus* must be regarded as a final renunciation. The opening of the *Historiae*, on which Tacitus worked from A.D. 106/7, unmistakably develops some themes from the *Dialogus*. This contemporary history (from the beginning of A.D. 69 to the death of Domitian) was followed by the *Annales* (*Ab excessu divi Augusti*), a history of the Julian and Claudian houses. Tacitus had planned also a history of Nerva and Trajan, but did not live to write it.

The *Agricola* is essentially a necrologue, enlarged to a bio-graphical-historical monograph, but much space is given to strictly historical matters. The main section, on Agricola's Britannic governorship, with its geographical and ethnographical opening and the great speeches of the leaders before the decisive battle, takes the form of a *bellum* in the manner of Sallust. In the *Agricola*, Tacitus had pictured a Roman of the old type against the background of a degenerate time; in the

Germania (*De origine et situ* or *De origine, situ, moribus ac populis Germanorum*) he strives for the understanding of a foreign way of life, in which he discovers all that gave power and greatness to the old Rome : *religio, virtus, simplicitas*, and above all *libertas* ; of a nation which, for those very reasons, can be a dangerous enemy of a Rome that has renounced her old virtues. The danger is all the greater because of the vast expansion of the Germanic tribes, who fade into the nebulous world of the extreme North and East.   Hence his dwelling on the contrast of contemporary civilization with ancient Roman and the Germany of his time.   Tacitus's picture of the ancient Germans is certainly tinged with a romantic idealization of the primitive, but he is not uncritical ; he sees the vices of the barbarians as clearly as the fundamental difference that the Roman is essentially a farmer, the German nothing but a warrior. Despite its similarity to the ethnological chapters in Posidonius, Caesar, Livy and others the *Germania* was certainly conceived from the beginning as an independent work. Even though Tacitus took over the topics and motifs of ancient ethnography (Herodotus had already, in a similar way, contrasted Greeks and Persians), his factual information appears to be on the whole accurate.

The *Dialogus de oratoribus* marks a turning-point in Tacitus's work. It is dedicated to Fabius Iustus (cos. suff. A.D. 102), and probably dates from the first years of the new century. Iustus had asked Tacitus to give his opinion on the causes of the decline of oratory ; he prefers to report a conversation, in which he had taken part as a young man — a similar literary fiction to that in Cicero's *De oratore*. The scene of the conversation is the house of the orator and tragic poet Curiatius Maternus ; the interlocutors, apart from Maternus, are the teachers of Tacitus, M. Aper and Iulius Secundus, and the then famous orator Messalla.   The discussion, which retains in some degree a conversational character, cleverly combines several related themes : the arts of poetry and oratory, the old and the new times, rhetoric and education, free speech and public order. These were then, as is known also from Quintilian, much-debated questions. Maternus holds that genuine eloquence inevitably died with the republic, but that the peace of the principate could be bought only at this price. Nerva and Trajan had succeeded in uniting what had seemed to be irreconcilable, principate and freedom (*Agr.* 3); but a wise, just, and moderate ruler is a rare blessing. And *virtus*, the responsible action of the citizen in the state, is possible only in freedom.

Such considerations as these lead to the threshold of Tacitus's great historical works, the *Annales* and *Historiae*. Written in the inverse order, they nevertheless form a whole : the *Annals* probably carried their subject to the point where the *Histories* begin. Although Tacitus, in annalistic fashion, records the events from year to year, he is, as in *Agricola* and *Germania*, primarily an interpreter and an artist. His style of historiography, which concentrates on great characters and momentous events and strives after an aesthetic effect analogous to that of tragedy, has a long tradition behind it. Polybius had argued against it, Cicero and Quintilian attempted to define its principle, and the annalists of the republic and of the empire cultivated it. It was the obvious form for Tacitus to choose. But for him art is not an end in itself ; it serves the purpose of historical interpretation. Tacitus thus follows in the footsteps of Sallust, not only in certain peculiarities of style and in his psychological characterization, but also in his use of irony, which for both writers is expressive of a serious moral attitude. Already the beginning of *Agricola* has a Sallustian ring. But the subject of Tacitus is greater : he is passing judgement on the principate as a form of government, not from the point of view of political theory but as a historical phenomenon. He rejects it on principle ; the recognition that it was inevitable makes this rejection even more bitter. But this is not said in so many words ; the reader is to deduce it from Tacitus's way of presenting the facts. Tacitus subjects him to every form of hidden persuasion : he does so by his selection of the facts, by his way of grouping and contrasting them, and above all by the art of discriminating by innuendo, of which he is the unrivalled master. Tacitus is certainly free from *ira* and *studium*, personal flattery and malice; he has, so he himself says, no cause for either. He could not and would not be unprejudiced in the sense of historical objectivity, and one must not reproach him for this. He writes as a citizen of Rome and as a senator. One charge, however, he cannot be spared: that he frequently casts suspicion on individual actions on the grounds of his overall interpretation of historic reality.

As Tacitus goes beyond Sallust as an historical thinker, so too he develops the latter's style — economy, brevity, solemnity and irony — to the utmost. This style becomes more and more tense as we go from the *Agricola* and *Germania* over the *Histories* to the first half of the *Annals*; in the last books (13–16) this tension is slightly relaxed.

6. The Later Period

ARCHAISM AND THE 'NEW SOPHISTIC'

WITH the emperor Hadrian (A.D. 117–138) there begins a new
era, the flourishing of a civilization founded on general prosperity, which is shared by the whole empire, East and West
alike. One of Hadrian's successors, Caracalla, was to give (in
A.D. 212) all free men of the empire Roman citizenship. Literary
culture extended over a still wider circle than in the first century,
but for all their zeal and good intentions no writer of that period
achieved greatness. Turning away from the literature of the
last hundred years, these poets and writers looked for models
among the early Augustans and even among the great authors
of the Republic. This was partly due to Greek influence, which
now began to reassert itself.

The seeds of Atticism had grown into the 'New Sophistic'
(apart from the name, it has only the emphasis on rhetoric in
common with the Greek sophists of the fifth century B.C.), in the
work of men like the wandering philosopher Dion of Prusa,
who delivered orations before Trajan, or the many-sided Lucian.
Plutarch (A.D. 45–125) in his parallel biographies had compared
famous Greeks with famous Romans; now Appianus from
Alexandria (a Roman knight under Hadrian) and, towards the
end of the century, the senator Cassius Dio (a relative of Dion
of Prusa) wrote Roman history in the Greek language. Even
men of the Latin West wrote Greek, *e.g.* Dion's pupil, the orator
Favorinus of Arelate (Arles), and A. Claudius Aelianus of
Praeneste (under Septimius Severus); both languages were
used by Suetonius, Fronto, Marcus Aurelius, Apuleius and the
Christian Tertullian. It is, to be sure, a coexistence rather than

G

a fusion: the Latin West and the Greek East were just then beginning to drift apart.

Archaism — the turning back to the pre-classic — is a general tendency of this period; it is most obvious, already under Hadrian, in the fine arts. In literature it does not gather momentum until the Antonines (A.D. 138–192).

Hadrian's private secretary C. SUETONIUS TRANQUILLUS, a typical civilian of the equestrian class, shared the wide interests of his royal employer. Of his extensive literary production, only little survives: some portion of the *Viri illustres* (*De grammaticis et rhetoribus* and individual *Vitae* from *De poetis* and *De historicis*) and the biographies of the emperors from Caesar to Domitian (*De vita Caesarum*), which are dedicated to the praetorian *praefectus* C. Septicius Clarus (A.D. 119–121). Suetonius dwells on the private life of the emperors (including court gossip). His interest in the person is characteristically Roman. The type of biography which Suetonius wrote set the fashion for many centuries to come.

For the use of the rhetorical schools a certain L. ANNAEUS FLORUS compiled an epitome of Livy. He is possibly the same Florus who wrote on the theme *Vergilius orator an poeta* and exchanged poetic letters with Hadrian. Two school-books on history, by Granius Licinianus and L. Ampelius, probably from the time of the Antonines, have also a limited value as sources.

The creator of the new style is M. CORNELIUS FRONTO from Cirta in Africa. As early as the reign of Hadrian he was an orator of some reputation; Antoninus Pius made him tutor to M. Aurelius and L. Verus, the heirs to the throne; in recognition of his services a consulate was bestowed on him in A.D. 143. We know Fronto best from his correspondence with M. Aurelius. He appears there as a great and beloved teacher, but also as a connoisseur of ancient literature and expert adviser on style. He did not recommend the hunt for archaic words at any price, but the search for the *mot juste*, which he hoped to find in the earlier Latin rather than in the later. Although he worshipped Cicero no less than Quintilian had done before him, his own style is dominated by that baroque rhetoric which was afterwards especially cultivated in Africa.

Among Fronto's friends were the orator Favorinus, the historian Appianus from Alexandria and the highly cultured Herodes Atticus, archon in Athens A.D. 125/126, famed as a teacher and orator, statesman and philanthropist, who perhaps best represents the culture of his time.

The influence of Fronto was felt strongly by A. GELLIUS, a man of universal interests, a lover of cultured and scholarly conversation. Much of this has gone into the twenty books of casual talk, to which, in memory of his year of study in Athens, he gave the title of *Noctes Atticae*. Gellius wrote in an artless, slightly archaic language — the language of a scholar. He is neither profound nor original, but a cultured man, for whom culture is an essential element of his life.

Of antiquarian content is the *De die natali* of Censorinus (A.D. 238). Grammatical studies also kept up a high standard. Let us mention Q. Terentius Scaurus, the author of an orthographical work and a commentary on Horace's *Ars poetica*; also the interpreters of Vergil, Velius Longus and Aemilius Asper; C. Sulpicius Apollinaris from Carthage, who besides technical works wrote metrical summaries of the books of the *Aeneid* and the plays of Terence; and Helenius Acro, who commented on Terence and Horace. Towards the end of the second century Terentianus Maurus (*i.e.* from Mauretania) wrote a handbook of metrics in verse.

Poetry too inclined towards the pre-classic, but shaped its models according to contemporary Greek technique. Only the official poem for the secular celebrations of the year A.D. 204, of which considerable fragments survive, conforms to classical conventions. The 'modern poets' favour miniature forms and aim at daintiness. Cases in point are the *Ruralia* of Septimius Serenus and the *Falisca* of Annianus. Occasionally ambitions would rise higher: one Alfius Avitus retold the whole of Roman history in iambics. In the second or third century belongs Vespa's *Iudicium coci et pistoris* (contest between cook and baker before Vulcan). The emperor Hadrian was a poetic *dilettante*; even the lines which he composed on his death-bed (*Animula vagula blandula . . .*) are in the manner of the 'new poetry'.

In the time of the Antonines fall the public appearances of APULEIUS from Madaura in Africa. His father was a high official; the son studied first in Carthage, then in Athens, and educated himself further through travel. For some time he was a lawyer in Rome, then he became a wandering orator. Extracts from his oratorical showpieces are the *Florida* in the lush 'African' style. More simple in tone is his *Apologia* before the proconsul of Africa, Claudius Maximus; having married a rich widow, he was accused by her relatives of having bewitched the woman with magic. Philosophical interests are betrayed in his *De deo Socratis*. (*De Platone et eius dogmate* and the translation of a Greek work *De mundo* are of doubtful authenticity.) Apuleius liked to call himself *philosophus Platonicus*; he is the earliest Latin witness to Neoplatonism. His place in world literature is due to his *Metamorphoses*, known under the title of *The Golden Ass*.

This novel in eleven books, modelled on a Greek work, describes the experiences of a young man, Lucius, who through the unsuspecting use of a charm is turned into an ass and after many vicissitudes regains his human form by eating roses at a procession in honour of Isis; he ends up as a *mystes* of the goddess. The longest episode, the story of Amor and Psyche, which an old woman tells a girl in distress to console her, is a genuine fairy tale, the only complete fairy tale known from antiquity. It begins in true fairy-tale manner ('There was once in a town a king and queen'), but this unfortunately gives way all too soon to the rhetorical style of the African. Many commentators have sought a mystical meaning in this tale, and have related it to Lucius's conversion to the worship of Isis. Apuleius (himself initiated into many mysteries) clearly identifies himself with his hero in the last book; the use of the first person, however, has led some interpreters into the error of regarding the whole novel as an allegorical autobiography.

With Hadrian begins the great period of Roman jurisprudence. At the suggestion of the emperor, Salvius Iulianus edited the praetorian edict that now became a law of the realm as *edictum perpetuum*. Under the Antonines (about A.D. 161) Gaius wrote the classical textbook of Roman law, the four books of *Institutiones*. Papinianus (under Septimius Severus), Ulpian and Paulus continued the tradition; large extracts from their writings are preserved in the *Digests* (*Pandects*) of Justinian's *Corpus Iuris* (A.D. 533/534). The language of these works is simple and follows the classical models.

One more work must be mentioned here, the 'Meditations' (*Eis heauton*), in Greek, of Marcus Aurelius, the philosopher-emperor. They not only form the most thought-provoking book that any Roman had written since Tacitus, but are also a landmark on the road of introspective writing from Cicero and Seneca to the 'Confessions' of Augustine.

ENTRY OF CHRISTIANITY INTO ROMAN LITERATURE

From the end of the second century there existed a Latin literature of Christianity. In the West the gospel was first spread principally among the Greek-speaking lower classes of the great cities. But in the course of the second century Latin established itself as the language of the western Church. This seems to have occurred first in Africa; here we find not only the earliest Latin translations of the Bible and of other early Christian writings, but also, with Tertullian and Cyprian of Carthage, the first original Christian literature in Latin; Tertullian's contemporary Minucius Felix, who wrote in Rome, was probably also an African.

The Christians' attitude to ancient literature was similar to that of the early Romans to the literature of the Greeks. Like the teaching of Jesus, that of his disciples was at first oral; only gradually did their oral style become literary. The inevitable conflict with the spirit and culture of hellenism, however, soon led to the adoption of its literary forms and their transformation in Christian spirit. Diatribe became apology, letter and speech became epistle and sermon, and philosophical didactic writing shaped the theological treatise; as the ancients had commented on their classics, so the Christians commented on the Bible. All this was primarily accomplished in the Greek church. The Latins at first went their own way: Tertullian's *Apologeticum* (A.D. 197) is a fictitious court speech, and the majority of his remaining works also show him as a lawyer; the writings and letters of the bishop Cyprian of Carthage (died A.D. 258) arose out of the practical problems of his episcopate. But the West for a long time had nothing similar to the great programme of a Christian culture (based on the ancient Paideia) which was outlined in the work of Clement of Alexandria (died before A.D. 215), Origen (died A.D. 254) and Eusebius of Caesarea (died after A.D. 337).

Christian Latin, in a wider sense, which transcends ecclesiastical Latin, developed as the 'group-language' of a community which, particularly in the times of persecution, was closely bound together. Formative influences included a conscious turning towards the spoken, popular language and the hellenistic Greek of the Bible with its Semitic background. The great ecclesiastical writers, who almost all, like the Greek fathers, had received rhetorical training, shaped it as a new literary language. The ground had been prepared by Tertullian, but the highly individual style of this most difficult of Latin authors did not recommend him as a model. In Cyprian the characteristics of Church Latin combine for the first time with elements of rhetoric to a slightly formal style of writing, which became the official language of bishops and popes, and (since Constantine) also of

Christian rulers. To some extent stylized rhetorical prose was cultivated, especially in Africa, where Augustine employed it with great effect in some of his sermons. Minucius Felix revived the Ciceronian dialogue with his *Octavius* (written after Tertullian's *Apologeticum*); Augustine did the same in the philosophical dialogues of the years A.D. 386–7. There were many Ciceronians among Christian writers, not only the 'Christian Cicero' Lactantius (about A.D. 300), whose chief work was the seven books *Divinarum institutionum*. The imitation of Cicero is not limited to the form: in the *Octavius* of Minucius Felix there is much of Cicero's *De natura deorum*; Ambrose deliberately created in *De officiis ministrorum* a counterpart to Cicero's *De officiis*.

In the time of crisis of the 'soldier emperors' — from the fall of the Severi (A.D. 235) to the election of Diocletian as emperor (A.D. 284) — Christian writers are almost the only ones to preserve a certain continuity of Latin literature; by contrast such a work as the compilation (*Collectanea*) of C. Iulius Solinus has value only because of some lost sources from which the compiler supplemented his main authority, Pliny the Elder.

LATIN LITERATURE FROM THE FOURTH CENTURY ONWARDS

The absolute monarchy of Diocletian and his successors, which with Constantine had taken the momentous step of entering into a union with the Church, gave cultural life a fresh incentive; the literary situation, however, had completely changed. Already during the third century the East and West had become increasingly estranged. Diocletian and Constantine tried to transplant Latin culture to the East; Diocletian, for example, called Lactantius, then still a pagan, from Africa to his court in Nicomedia. But the process of separation went on; the division of the empire in A.D. 395 set the seal on it. The Roman empire was no longer bilingual; it consisted of a Greek and a Latin half; and in the West the knowledge of Greek was limited to ever narrower circles.

As a result, the West was flooded with translations. In the fourth century Chalcidius translated Plato's *Timaeus* together with a neo-platonic commentary; C. Marius Victorinus, who later became a Christian, translated works of Plato, Aristotle and Porphyry. Most frequent were translations of Christian literature: biblical commentaries, homilies, and lives of saints. Euagrius translated Athanasius's *Vita S. Antonii* (about A.D. 370), Rufinus of Aquileia and Jerome translated works of Origen and Eusebius. Most important is the revision of the Latin Bible, which Jerome undertook at the suggestion of Pope Damasus. This 'Vulgate' (*Vulgata*) began as a revision of the psalms and the New Testament on the basis of Greek texts; the proto-canonical books of the Old Testament were translated directly from the Hebrew.

In poetry the gulf between Christians and pagans gradually narrows. Christian themes are treated in classical form, as in the gospel-epic of Iuvencus, or in the poems of Prudentius and Sedulius; and Christians like Ausonius or Sidonius Apollinaris make use of ancient mythology in profane poems as a poetic convention. Religious poetry in a more specific sense is repre-sented by the Ambrosian hymns, in four-line iambic stanzas, in which rhythm and word-accent tend to coincide. There also emerged a verse of new type, based on a mere count of syllables, which corresponded to the structure of spoken late Latin, as in Augustine's fighting song against the Donatists (*Psalmus contra partem Donati*). A strange hybrid of 'old' and 'new' versification is the hexameter of Commodianus. However, the classical forms of poetry and prose, with which the living language had long since broken, were preserved by a school tradition which has continued into modern times.

There had been a hard battle between the old and the new. It was, however, decided before it had begun: the traditionalists merely tried to hold an obsolete position; for the Christians, the most vital issues of human existence were at stake. In the East the pagan reaction found an enthusiastic champion in the emperor Julian, the last ruler of the house of Constantine. In the West, its heart was the senate; the transfer of the imperial residence to Milan, Treves or Ravenna, and in the East to Nicomedia (after A.D. 330 to Constantinople), gave the senate in Rome a new importance as a corporate body, but directed its thoughts ever more towards the past greatness of the now politically insignificant city. Of the Christian Rome, which just at that time was represented by a man of such intellectual stature as Pope Damasus, little notice was taken in those circles.

Typical of this attitude are the seven books of *Saturnalia* of MACROBIUS THEODOSIUS (about A.D. 400), conceived in clear imitation of the framework of Cicero's *Republic* (on its final section, the *Somnium Scipionis*, Macrobius also wrote a commentary). The *Saturnalia* consist of conversations, at the Saturnalian festival, between the leading senators of the time (including Nicomachus Flavianus and the orator Q. Aurelius Symmachus) and the grammarian Servius, on antiquarian themes, especially on Vergil. Symmachus, in a speech in A.D. 384, which became famous, had asked the emperor Valentinian II to restore the altar of Victoria, which had recently been removed by Gratian from the senate-house; but bishop Ambrose prevailed upon the emperor to refuse the petition. It is characteristic that both opponents introduced the personified Roma, Symmachus as the embodiment of tradition, Ambrose as the symbol of an empire that had become Christian. It was a test case, which made a great impression. As late as A.D. 400, when the statue (not the altar) of the goddess of victory was set up again in the senate by Stilicho, Prudentius in his poem *Contra Symmachum*, took up the Ambrosian idea of Rome. Ambrose and Prudentius had been high officials; in both the old Roman spirit lives on, but it has been christened.

To a man of the pagan reaction we owe the last great work of Roman historiography. AMMIANUS MARCELLINUS from Antioch was an officer under Constantine and Julian: he later ettled in Rome and wrote there a continuation of the histories of Tacitus (*Rerum gestarum libri*), from Nerva to Valens (A.D. 96–378); books 18–31, which deal with contemporary history, survive. The stylistic imitation of Tacitus is evident, but the Greek mother-tongue of Ammianus often rings through. He does not stand up to his model in depth of thought and psychological penetration, but surpasses him in breadth of vision and, with all his admiration for Julian, in objectivity.

Christian historiography is well represented by SULPICIUS SEVERUS (*Chronica*, completed in A.D. 403); to the middle ages, however, he was known best as the author of the St. Martin legend. The Spaniard PAULUS OROSIUS, in his *Historiae adversus paganos* (before A.D. 417), drew his material hastily from various sources (*e.g.* the Livy epitome); he wrote history with an apologetic purpose. Unique among the historical sources for this period is the *Commemoratorium* concerning St. Severin, the apostle of Noricum Ripense (d. 482), written by his former companion EUGIPPIUS in 511.

Most historical writing of the fourth entury is insignificant. The *Caesares* of Aurelius Victor (A.D. 360), reaching as far as Constantius, are at least taken from good sources; the anonymous work *De viris illustribus urbis Romae* also gives some valuable information. Of less value is the *Origo gentis Romanae*, handed down in the same manuscript, and the so-called *Historia Augusta* (biographies of the emperors from Hadrian to Diocletian A.D. 117–285, with gaps), allegedly written under Constantine but probably in the time of Theodosius, certainly after A.D. 360/361. The *Breviarium ab urbe condita* (ten books) of Eutropius (under Valens), though not original, is well and intelligently written. Mention must be made also of the *Epitoma rei militaris* (four books) of Flavius Vegetius Renatus (fifth century); with these extracts from earlier historians and strategists he hoped to check the decay of Roman military art. Vegetius is also the author of a competent veterinary work (*Mulomedicina*).

The official rhetoric of the third and fourth centuries is known to us from a collection of panegyrics by rhetors of Gaul. Some of these speeches are of interest to the historian of culture, *e.g.*, the speech of Eumenius (A.D. 297) on the reconstruction of the schools of Autun, or the New Year oration (A.D. 362) of consul Mamertinus before Julian in Constantinople. Letter-writing increases vastly. We still possess the collected correspondence of such men as Symmachus or Sidonius Apollinaris, and, on the Christian side, of Cyprian, Jerome, Augustine and Pope Leo I. The novel also is well represented. The Latin adaptation by one L. Septimius (in the time of Constantine) of the 'Trojan War' of the mythical Cretan Dictys is followed in the fifth century by that of its pendant, allegedly by a Phrygian, Dares. Though of no literary value, these much-read works became the sources of the mediaeval Troy legend. A Christian novel, the *Recognitiones*, was translated into Latin by Rufinus. Touched up by a Christian revisor is the *Historia Apollonii regis Tyri* (cf. Shakespeare's 'Pericles, Prince of Tyre') ; it already foreshadows the mediaeval romances.

Well-known grammarians of the period are AELIUS DONA-TUS, who, apart from two grammars (the *Ars minor* and the *Ars maior*), wrote commentaries on Terence and Vergil; also Charisius, Diomedes, the Vergil commentator Servius and the African Priscianus (about A.D. 500, in Constantinople). The middle ages learned Latin principally from these works; 'Donatus' came to be synonymous with 'Grammar'.

Compendia of the *artes liberales* begin to take on the form in which they were known in the middle ages. A complete compendium is the *De nuptiis Mercurii et Philologiae* of the North African MARTIANUS CAPELLA (about A.D. 400) ; the dull material is presented in a fantastic frame: Mercury marries Philology and, as a bridal gift, gives her seven girls, the seven *artes*, who then, one after the other, recite their lessons. The mixture of prose and verse makes the work formally a *Menippea* ; the language, however, now dry and technical, now baroque and rhetorical, is far from that of the *Satura*. This did not affect the success of the work as a textbook ; from the ninth century onwards Martianus Capella is one of the authors most widely read and most frequently expounded.

Poetry takes a promising turn with the *Pervigilium Veneris*. In the popular *versus quadratus* with a recurrent line (*Cras amet qui numquam amavit, quique amavit cras amet*), fluently written, it describes a festival of Venus with attractive nature-images and scenes of playful activities. The poem was composed probably bout A.D. 307 in Nicomedia in the circle of Romula, mother of the emperor Galerius; the poet might have been an African, who like Lactantius was called to the eastern court; the final lines of his poem have a nostalgic ring.

The figure-poems of Optatianus Porfyrius (under Constantine) deserve a passing mention, as does Tiberianus, who occupied high offices between A.D. 326 and 335, and is probably the author of several poems handed down under this name, among them a fine nature poem and a neoplatonic prayer or hymn similar to that in the *Consolatio* of Boethius. The distinguished Rufius Festus Avienus wrote *Phaenomena* after Aratos; one of his geographical poems, *Ora maritima* (coast description of the Mediterranean, in iambics), is valuable to the historian because it makes use of very old Greek sources. In the circle of Symmachus originated the collection of epigrams of Naucellius and his friends. As a Christian counterpart there are the epigrams, mostly in hexameters, of Pope Damasus, largely sepulchral inscriptions for apostles, martyrs and popes. About A.D. 400 Symphosius composed his poetic riddles (*Enigmas*); they influenced Aldhelm of Malmesbury and other Anglo-Saxons.

A greater talent was D. MAGNUS AUSONIUS, professor of rhetoric in Burdigala (Bordeaux), then teacher of Prince Gratian, under whose reign he was consul in A.D. 379; after Gratian's death (A.D. 383) he withdrew to his home where he died in A.D. 395. His poems give a good picture of the contemporary world, drawn by an educated Christian layman. Yet there was no room in his life for the counsels of Christian perfection. That his pupil and friend Paulinus, a gifted poet and orator (died A.D.

431 as bishop of Nola), should renounce the world, was beyond his comprehension.

In his best known poem, *Mosella*, Ausonius describes a journey along the Moselle to Treves; here in the form of a hymn to the river-deity an *iter* is combined with a rhetorical description of the river. With evident love, Ausonius depicts the life on its banks, and vividly describes a boat-race. His catalogue poems, like *Ordo nobilium urbium* (with a place of honour for Bordeaux), or the *Commemoratio professorum Burdigalensium*, have a certain interest, as has the *Cento nuptialis*; although it includes an over-explicit description of the wedding night, it consists entirely of Vergilian lines and half-lines. (At about the same time a Roman lady named Proba described the gospel story in such a Vergilian verse-mosaic.)

A genuine poet is CLAUDIUS CLAUDIANUS, of Alexandria (died after A.D. 404). He went to the court of the emperor Honorius and wrote epics of contemporary history (*e.g. De bello Gotico*, A.D. 402) and pieces of invective, modelled on Juvenal, against ministers of the Eastern Empire (*In Rufinum*, A.D. 396; *In Eutropium*, A.D. 399). He became the herald of the policy of Stilicho, the Vandal, who in the spirit of Roman tradition until his tragic end worked for the union of the divided empire. A mythological epic *De raptu Proserpinae* remained incomplete. Claudian was a nominal Christian, and wrote also the (commissioned) poem *De Salvatore* ('About the Saviour'). As he renewed the satire of Juvenal in his own manner, so also, in his epics, is he heir to Vergil and Ovid, Lucan and Statius. His language and verse-technique are remarkable for their classical purity; and mythology, even in his contemporary epics is still for him a living poetic force.

In A.D. 404/405 the Spaniard AURELIUS PRUDENTIUS CLEMENS, then in his fifty-seventh year, edited a collection of his poems. Of the lyric pieces in various metres and stanzas (*e.g.* the *Peristephanon*, hymns of praise for martyrs), some have found their way into liturgy. Among the didactic poems in hexameters, the *Psychomachia*, the struggle of the personified virtues and vices for the human soul, became most famous. The poem moves on several planes, and interweaves realistic scenes of combat, Biblical *exempla* and allegorical interpretations. Illustrated soon after it had been written, the *Psychomachia* had great influence on the virtue-and-vice allegories of the middle ages. A poet of great vigour and passion, Prudentius foreshadows the spirit and temperament of the Spanish baroque.

Quite different in spirit is the poetic *iter* of the Gaul RUTILIUS CLAUDIUS NAMATIANUS, *magister officiorum* and city prefect of Rome. He describes a journey to his native country which he made in A.D. 416 or 417 in order to look after his estates which had been laid waste by the Goths: *De reditu suo* (two books) in elegiac couplets, surviving incomplete. Masterly control of form is combined with great vividness and a lively temperament. Although probably a Christian, Rutilius was deeply attached to ancient Rome, of whose mission he did not despair even after the occupation and plundering of Rome by Alaric (A.D. 410); his farewell hymn addressed to Rome, the *regina mundi* (I, 47–164), is a moving profession of loyalty. His aversion to monasticism, which had recently penetrated from the East into the Western Mediterranean and to which he himself had 'lost' a distinguished young friend, was then shared by many Christians; but the criticism of Rutilius is especially bitter and is levelled not only against monasticism as an extreme form of Christian life, but against the spirit out of which it grew.

The fall of Rome in A.D. 410 gave Augustine (AURELIUS AUGUSTINUS, A.D. 354–430) the impetus to write his most influential work, the twenty-two books of the *De civitate Dei*. Born at Tagaste as the son of a pagan father and a Christian mother, he was brought up a Christian, but turned away from Christianity during his studies in Carthage; after a troubled spiritual development as a Manichean, sceptic and neoplatonic, his eyes were opened to the spirit of Christianity by Ambrose in Milan, who in A.D. 387 baptized him. After a period of philosophical and religious contemplation, he returned home; in A.D. 395 he became bishop of Hippo. In his *Confessiones* (about A.D. 400), a confession before God in the form of a passionate prayer, he described in retrospect, also with a view to his contemporaries, his own way to the acceptance of the Christian revelation.

Augustine was a thinker of exceptional originality, as he had already proved in his youthful *Dialogues* and *Soliloquia*. The frequent reproach, that the evils of the time were due to the rejection of the ancient gods and the victory of Christianity, prompted him to a penetrating discussion of what Rome had stood for. Rome is no symbol to him as to Symmachus, Claudian or Prudentius, but only a great historical power which he analyses critically. The forces which determine history are, according to him, the two opposed kingdoms, the earthly and the heavenly. They grow in this life in an insoluble tangle; not until the end of time will the victory of God's kingdom become definite.

The fifth century saw the dissolution of the Western Empire as a political structure. The Visigoths ruled from A.D. 415 in Southern Gaul (until, in A.D. 507, they moved on to Spain); the Vandals, who at the time of Augustine's death were besieging Hippo, established themselves in Africa; at the end of the century (A.D. 493) Theodoric founded the sixty-year rule of the Ostrogoths in Italy. In the general collapse of culture it is again the senatorial landowners who by their care for Rome's intellectual heritage prevented a complete rupture in literary tradition.

To them belonged the highly educated Gaul C. SOLLIUS APOLLINARIS SIDONIUS, who was even thoroughly conversant with Greek; not only did he successfully put the case of his countrymen before several emperors in rhetorical poems of praise and with clever diplomacy, but later, as Bishop of Clermont (from A.D. 470), despite many humiliations, managed to mediate between the Galloromans and their Gothic masters.

His poems have little aesthetic appeal. The nine books of his letters, in a stilted rhetorical style, give an interesting picture of contemporary society. If Sidonius shared the prejudices of his class, he was, within these limitations, high-minded and likeable.

Africa did not begin to recover intellectually until the end of the century. Under King Gunthamund (A.D. 484–496), BLOSSIUS AEMILIUS DRACONTIUS from Carthage wrote occasional poems, among them the *Satisfactio*, a plea of the imprisoned poet for pardon, mythological epics and a poem *De laudibus Dei* (book I, on the creation, has poetic merit). Dracontius is probably also the author of the *Orestis tragoedia*; from the same circle emanated the epyllion *Aegritudo Perdiccae* (Perdiccas, for his neglect of Venus, is punished by Cupid with sensual love for his own mother, and dies in the conflict between his passion and his moral sense). LUXORIUS, in the sixth century, is the last of a line of poets whose products, along with earlier pieces like the *Pervigilium Veneris*, make up the Latin Anthology (originally in twenty-four books). About A.D. 550 FLAVIUS CRESCONIUS CORIPPUS glorified in his *Iohannis* (eight books) the Moorish campaign of the Byzantine general Iohannes. Later he held a court office in Byzantium; in his old age he wrote the *In laudem Iustini*. In the earlier work Corippus is a sympathetic chronicler, who knows how to tell a good story.

The Ostrogoth Theodoric (A.D. 493–526) gave Italy a last brief spell of material prosperity and intellectual culture. He left civil administration in the hands of the Roman upper class; he also took a keen interest in their intellectual preoccupations. To this class belonged MAGNUS AURELIUS CASSIODORUS, (cos. A.D. 514). He was secretary of state under Theodoric and his successors before he retired to his southern Italian estate and as abbot of Vivarium tried to realize, on a small scale, the unfulfilled dream of his life, a Christian university.

Of his numerous writings the *Variae* (collection of official letters, twelve books) are indispensable for the political, the *Institutiones* (two books) for the cultural history of the times.

His Gothic History would be of still greater interest; unfortunately we only know it in the extract of a contemporary, the Romanized Goth Iordanes.

Along with Cassiodorus, ENNODIUS must be named (died A.D. 521 as Bishop of Ticinum), in verse and prose a not unworthy representative of the classical Christian tradition. His protégé ARATOR wrote an allegorical epic *De actibus apostolorum* and read it to a distinguished audience at Rome in A.D. 544 with great success.

Most important in the field of literature was ANICIUS MANLIUS SEVERINUS BOETHIUS (cos. A.D. 510, then *magister officiorum*). In full possession of Greco-Roman culture, both national and Christian, he was convinced of the fundamental unity of Platonic-Aristotelian and Christian doctrine. Besides the duties of the high offices to which the king called him, Boethius found time for extensive scholarly writing. He entered the dogmatic disputes of the time as an orthodox theologian. His great plan to translate and comment on the whole of Plato and Aristotle and to prove their essential agreement never got beyond the beginnings (translation and explanation of the Aristotelian *Organon* and the *Isagoge* of Porphyry). In A.D. 523 Boethius, not yet forty-five years old, was suspected of high treason with Byzantium, found guilty by the intimidated senate, and was executed in the following year. In the *Consolation of Philosophy*, written between trial and execution, Boethius gave his personal philosophy a mature form.

The five books *De philosophiae consolatione*, like the work of Martianus Capella, are in form a *Satura Menippea*. In content, they are a self-consolation, or rather a *protrepticus*, addressed by the author to himself. Boethius follows largely Cicero's *Hortensius* and its Aristotelian model; but as Augustine gave his *Soliloquia* the form of a dialogue between himself and *Ratio*, so the *Consolatio* is a dialogue between Boethius and personified Philosophy. After the sick spirit of Boethius, through the 'weaker remedy' of cynic and stoic diatribe, has learnt to realize

the unreasonableness of his complaints and the worthlessness of
the earthly goods he has lost, the 'stronger remedies' of Platonic
and Aristotelian metaphysics and theology remind him of his
immortal nature, destined to unity with God, which can be
recognized already in this life as inner freedom from the compulsion of fate. The climax of the work is a solemn hymn to the
creator of the world, as conceived in Plato's *Timaeus* and his
neoplatonic exponents. The remaining poems, in various
metres, put into verse the thoughts of the prose chapters, and
illustrate them from mythology and history, or else are personal,
like the moving elegy at the beginning. Poetically they are of
uneven value. Mythology is here integrated into the Christian
world; it is neither allegory nor just a literary device, but par-
able. Boethius keeps strictly within the philosophical frame he
has chosen. There is not a word of Christ, grace, salvation, and
only searching interpretation reveals links with Augustinian
theology. Boethius has a deep and passionate feeling for the
great philosophical questions: the worthlessness of earthly goods,
the meaning of life, immortality, providence, chance and free
will. These questions are here put with an urgency which
makes the book a work of world literature.

Soon after Boethius's death the reconquest of Italy by
Byzantium and the desperate resistance of the Ostrogoths hit
prosperity and culture hard. However, the classical heritage
was not lost; men like Cassiodorus in the South and the Irish-
man Columbanus in the North preserved it, and in the Spanish
Visigothic kingdom it survived to the end of the seventh
century. The poetry of Venantius Fortunatus (born about A.D.
530 near Treviso, died soon after A.D. 600 as bishop of Poitiers)
also forms a bridge to the middle ages. When the schools of
Charlemagne took possession of the Roman heritage, Boethius
was rightly regarded as the last great representative of Roman
literature.

INDEX

PRINTED BY R. & R. CLARK, LTD., EDINBURGH